Galatians

The Gospel According to Paul

David K. Huttar

CHRISTIAN PUBLICATIONS, INC.
CAMP HILL, PENNSYLVANIA

Christian Publications, Inc.
3825 Hartzdale Drive, Camp Hill, PA 17011
www.cpi-horizon.com
www.christianpublications.com

Faithful, biblical publishing since 1883

Galatians
ISBN: 0-87509-922-X

LOC Control Number: 00-135129

Lovingly dedicated to my wife

Ethel Joy Kaiser Huttar,

faithful companion and helper,

who labored in the marketplace

nearly forty years

that I might pursue

the cloistered academic life

Contents

Foreword

We live in a day in which various groups have been writing statements defining the gospel of Jesus Christ. Perhaps it began with the Lausanne Covenant or the later Chicago Statement on Biblical Inerrancy. One that caused much debate was presented by evangelicals and Catholics together. When *Christianity Today* published "The Gospel of Jesus Christ: An Evangelical Celebration," many evangelicals enthusiastically endorsed it.

There are at least two reasons for this effort to define the gospel. There is a desire on the one hand to bring as much unity as possible in the Christian community. At the same time, the statements must be clear enough to protect the gospel from heresy and differentiate it from that presented by false cults.

For David Huttar, the theme of the book of Galatians is *the gospel*. His book reflects Paul's desire "that the truth of the *gospel* might remain with you" (Galatians 2:5, italics added). That means that the gospel must be presented in an authoritative way while condemning those who would add to it, distort it or pervert it.

Huttar uses the whole book of Galatians to do that and more. For the gospel is not only the good news that brings salvation to all men, but it also contains in it guidance and power for the Christian life as well. Some complain that recent statements on the gospel major on justification and are weak on sanctification. This is not true of Dr. Huttar's work. He ties in every aspect of the Christian life to the gospel. The same good news which produces life in the believer also guides him into the deeper life—the abundant life—as well. Thus Huttar writes intensely of the need for fervent belief in and earnest proclamation of God's message. So this is not only a book to guide the reader into doctrinal correctness, but also one which shows the privileges and responsibilities of the Christian as well.

This volume is both for the new Christian and for the more mature. It is readable and holds one's attention, but not at the expense of scholarly research. Further, the author searches far and wide, both in Scripture and elsewhere, for illustrations to show that Paul's teaching is not some novelty or aberration.

Huttar, a graduate of Wheaton College and Brandeis University, is a person of spiritual and mental integrity. He has always been willing to ask the hard questions so that the ground of his belief would be not only the writings of others but also based on his own personal convictions. I saw this in the years I was his pastor. Since then he has for years served at Nyack College as professor and now also as Executive Assistant to the President. And when he speaks of the deeper life as being a part of the content of the gospel, he is speaking of truth he has experienced.

Those who live in the shelter of churches and institutions in which the gospel is rarely challenged need to remember that in every age the gospel is under attack in one way or another. In Paul's day the greatest attack was the effort of those in the church to add Jewish works to the free gift of Christ. This could not be allowed. Legalism is still a problem today, but now with the many attempts to accommodate various groups there is also the danger of compromising the gospel to bring as much agreement as possible. Unity is always admirable, but never at the expense of perverting the gospel. Huttar's book shows he does not believe Paul would ever be a part of that.

Donald A. Miller
St. Louis, MO

GALATIANS

Acknowledgments

A glance at the Select Bibliography at the end of this volume will indicate that my chief indebtedness is to commentaries by evangelical scholars of the last two decades. Although I know none of these authors personally, I have enjoyed interacting with their ideas and arguments, more often than not accepting the conclusions of one or another of them. My book is different from theirs in purpose and cannot compete with them in depth of coverage. They are recommended for further study.

Interaction with my Nyack College colleagues, some of whom I have worked with for more years than one would like to admit, has been another invaluable source for the development of my ideas and perspectives. Of these I wish to mention in particular Dr. Donal E. Nilsson, Dr. Eldon Woodcock, Dr. Elio Cuccaro and Prof. Thomas N. Donworth. I also wish to thank Dr. Cuccaro for encouraging me to undertake this project on Galatians and for prompting me to meet many deadlines along the way.

In addition to these colleagues, I owe much in the way of intellectual stimulation to my brother-in-law, Dr. Walter C. Kaiser, Jr., and my two brothers, Dr. Charles A. Huttar and Dr. George L. Huttar, all of whom have spent their respective careers interacting with the text of Holy Scripture.

At Christian Publications, Janet Dixon has been most helpful in guiding me through the editorial process. Without her, the work would surely not have come to a satisfactory conclusion.

Finally, there is a debt that is owed to all those faithful believers who put into practice the message of Galatians, thus inspiring us all to probe its meaning and implications for Christian living. One example of such an outlook is the AWHO (As We Have Opportunity [Galatians 6:10]) Sunday school class of Folcroft (PA) Union Church.

Galatians: The Book of Paul's Gospel

Galatians 1:1-5

Paul, an apostle—sent not from men nor by man, but by Jesus Christ and God the Father, who raised him from the dead—and all the brothers with me,
To the churches in Galatia:
Grace and peace to you from God our Father and the Lord Jesus Christ, who gave himself for our sins to rescue us from the present evil age, according to the will of our God and Father, to whom be glory for ever and ever. Amen.

Many years ago a team of evangelists was preaching the gospel in a key city in the southern Balkans and was meeting with phenomenal success under the blessing of the Lord. But then the evangelists and their converts ran into some stiff opposition from an influential segment of the population, so much so that the evangelistic team felt it best to leave town and hope that the new converts would remain true to their profession of faith in Christ. The city was Thessalonica, and the evangelists Paul, Silas and Timothy (Acts 17:1-10).

As the weeks passed, Paul, the leader, became extremely anxious to hear what had become of these Thessalonian believers. Had they held fast to the gospel message? Or had they, under persecution from their fellow townspeople, slipped back into their old pre-Christian ways? He awaited the news with much anticipation. Finally, the news came, and it was good news indeed. Listen to his experience as he tells it in his own words recorded in his first letter to these dear friends:

> But, brothers, when we were torn away from you for a short time (in person, not in thought), out of our intense longing we made every effort to see you. For we wanted to come to you—certainly I, Paul, did, again and again—but Satan stopped us. . . . When I could stand it no longer, I sent to find out about your faith. I was afraid that in some way the tempter might have tempted you and our efforts might have been useless.
>
> But Timothy has just now come to us from you and has brought good news about your faith and love. (1 Thessalonians 2:17-18; 3:5-6)

What wonderful news this was, and what rejoicing there must have been!

Probably everyone has experienced the excitement and joy of receiving good news. Perhaps a loved one has gone on a journey and the family anxiously awaits the good news of a safe arrival at the anticipated destination. Or you may be anxious about a friend's medical test, and there comes the good news that the condition is benign. Or perhaps you have taken an exam—for entrance into college, or as a part of qualifying for a job—and again are relieved when you receive the good news of success. Such a sense of joy and satisfaction is well expressed in the proverb, "Like cold water to a weary soul is good news from a distant land" (Proverbs 25:25).

So it is with the good news of the gospel. To anyone burdened with a sense of sin and guilt before God, the gospel affords relief and refreshing. Its offer of pardon and cleansing from sin and peace with God is good news indeed. And while the whole New Testament gives expression to this gospel of God's grace to undeserving sinners, it may be that the relatively small book of Galatians contains its most concentrated treatment. Paul's letter to the Galatian Christians is preeminently the book of the gospel and therefore deserves careful and diligent consideration. What is this book that we may appropriately refer to as the book of Paul's gospel?

By way of introduction, we may first briefly consider its form. It is interesting that the writer to the Hebrews began his book by drawing attention to the fact that the Revealer-God chose to present His truth "in various ways" (Hebrews 1:1). This is, of course, precisely what we find throughout the history of God's redemptive activity. Without a doubt, God's truth comes to us in the Scriptures by means of many books, and these books are of many different literary forms and types— story, law, psalm, vision, letter, etc. Among all these various kinds of literature found in Scripture, the book of Galatians stands, of course, as a letter. As such it has several interesting characteristics.

When compared with some of the letters in the New Testament, it is relatively brief—brief enough to be read easily in one sitting and brief enough that one can read it again and again, from one perspective and another, pondering its interlocking themes and emphases.

It is a personal letter, though not in the sense of what it reveals of its first *readers*. We know next to nothing about them as individuals. Perhaps because it is written to several churches in an area ("the *churches* in Galatia"), it contains no greetings to individuals by name or even greetings from Paul's associates in ministry, as is the case in several others of Paul's letters.[1]

On the other hand, while the original audience remains largely anonymous, the letter is personal in what it reveals of the *writer.* It shows its author as defensive, as passionately concerned for the gospel and those who have embraced it, as intensely striving to spell out the logical implications of the gospel message.

But to say simply that this book is a letter is still not sufficient to grasp its essential nature. After all, there are many different kinds of letters—Christmas letters, prayer letters, love letters, etc. The book of Galatians is none of these. Rather, it is a letter in which the author sought to give his advice on a very touchy personal subject, when the advice had not been solicited.

It is hard to think of a comparable experience in our everyday life. Certainly, such a letter would carry with it a great deal of risk that the recipients would not accept the advice at all and would be turned off completely from what the author was trying to accomplish. In Paul's case, however, he at least had the advantage of having previously been the recipients' spiritual mentor and friend, albeit for only a short time. And during that short period, the Galatians had seen firsthand Paul's true love and concern for them. That ought to have made the reception of this controversial letter a little more palatable to them.

This gem of the New Testament is an open invitation for us as well to enter into consideration of the heart of the Bible's concern—the gospel of salvation by grace. And our diligent response to this invitation will certainly receive abundant blessing from the Revealer-God who stands behind the human author's efforts. Let us, then, as we enter this study, give preliminary attention to three aspects of the book of Galatians: its influence, its background and its message.

Its Influence

It should be fairly obvious to anyone familiar with the history of the church from Reformation to modern times that this little book has had influence far in excess of its size. We could think of its role in the thinking of Martin Luther and his emphasis on justification by faith. Beyond this, we may think of the verses from the book that are very dear to believers. Even when they may not necessarily be able to associate them with this book itself, believers through the centuries have found to be very precious and challenging verses such as the following:

- I am crucified with Christ.

- Bear one another's burdens.

- The fruit of the Spirit is love, joy, peace . . .

- In Christ there is neither Jew nor Greek, slave nor free, male nor female.

- It is for freedom that Christ has set us free.

- A man reaps what he sows.

- As we have opportunity . . .

- Serve one another in love.

- God sent the Spirit of His Son into our hearts.

But was this book always popular? We might suppose that it was not; that attention to the longer book of Romans, treating similar themes in a seemingly more systematic fashion, might have overshadowed interest in Galatians; that a letter such as Galatians, not specifically associated with the Christian community of a large city, might have been overlooked in favor of books like Romans, Corinthians or Ephesians.

This was apparently not the case. J.B. Lightfoot, the noted nineteenth-century evangelical British scholar of Pauline studies, stated in his review of ancient commentaries on Galatians that perhaps there were more patristic commentaries on this book than on any other Pauline epistle.[2] So while the early Church seems to have given more attention to the gospel records of Christ than to other blocks of New Testament literature, as far as the Pauline corpus is concerned, Galatians maintained its own as a document to be studied and cherished. Indeed, this can be shown to be the case from as early as the letters of Ignatius of Antioch and Polycarp, barely after the close of the New Testament, in which fairly clear echoes of Galatians are to be found.[3]

Its Background (1:1-2)

Normally when we read a book of the Bible (or any other book, for that matter), we rightly think it will help our understanding if we know something about its author, its intended readers and its setting, the circumstances for which it was written.

In response to this interest, we take up our study of Galatians with a consideration of its first five verses. These are something of an introduction to the book as a whole and are cast in a form typical of the introduction to an ancient letter, and particularly of Christian letters. First there is an indication of the sender and the addressees.

In regard to the first of these concerns—the sender of the letter—we are fortunately on solid ground. There has never been any significant doubt that the Apostle Paul, the great early convert to Christianity out of Judaism, was the writer of Galatians. Only the most liberal and radical New Testament critics have denied its authorship by Paul;[4] most scholars, however, have seen it as the one most indisputably Pauline document. We therefore may likewise proceed on that basis without further discussion.

At the same time, we note that Paul includes as the senders of the letter, at least in a formal sense, his companions in ministry ("all the brothers with me") or perhaps even the Christians who lived in the area from which he was writing. In either case, there is no reason to think that "brothers" was being used so restrictively as to rule out a reference to women. They must have been included under the second option (all Christians in the area) and may well have been part of Paul's ministry team if the first alternative is correct. We do not, however, have a very clear idea of just where the place of writing was.

The letter's authorship may be beyond dispute, but when it comes to the original readers, it is a different matter. It all depends on what is meant by the term "Galatia," an elusive term indeed. Linguistically, the term "Galatia" is related to such widely separated peoples as the Gauls of France and the Celts of the British islands and of Central Europe. In relation to the book of Galatians, however, the choice is far narrower: Does it refer to what may be called "ethnic" Galatia, an area in the central to northern part of what is now Turkey? Or does it mean "provincial" Galatia, the Roman province of Galatia south of "ethnic" Galatia? Thus we have what are known as the North Galatian and South Galatian theories regarding the identity of the first readers.

According to the first view, Paul would be writing presumably to converts he had brought to Christ on his "second missionary journey."[5] According to the second view, the recipients of the letter are those he had evangelized in Iconium, Lystra and Derbe on his "first missionary journey," narrated in Acts 14:1-20. Despite the debate involved in this thorny issue, we will simply adopt the latter theory, the one that in any event seems to be receiving increasing support and acceptance.

As for the letter's setting, unfortunately any decision on the specific setting, circumstances and date of the epistle is usually felt to be intertwined with one's decision in regard to the identity of the original readers. Thus, those who prefer the South Galatian view of the recipients will often argue that Galatians was an early letter, perhaps Paul's earliest, written before the Jerusalem Council (narrated in Acts 15) that took place between Paul's first and second journeys. On the other hand, those who opt for the Northern identity of the Galatians typically see the book as considerably later in Paul's career, associating it with the book of Romans, which is similar in theme.[6]

There is, however, a mediating position that does not link together the two issues of destination and date in the traditional way. This view holds that the letter was written to the Christians in the southern area, but after the Council of Jerusalem, rather than before it.[7] This is a very attractive solution to the problem and the one we will accept provisionally in order to work with the text.

With the uncertainties involved, it appears that we cannot reconstruct a very specific set of circumstances that Paul was addressing. Even some aspects of the false teaching that he found it necessary to combat are elusive. We can, however, be sure that he was writing to a group of churches personally established by him that were subsequently being threatened with some kind of false teaching.[8]

Its Message (Galatians 1:3-5)

Whatever we might conclude about Galatians' influence and background, probably most of us would say that what really matters more than these things is the book's message, and that message becomes evident as our text continues with the author's opening prayer for his readers. While these verses are to some extent the formulaic beginning of a first-century epistle, it is also obvious that the writer has already begun to plunge into his grand theme of the gospel of salvation. Notice the various elements of Christian teaching contained in these few seemingly casual lines.

First of all, when Paul prays that grace and peace would come to his readers from both God our Father and the Lord Jesus Christ, there is the association of God the Father and Jesus Christ in a way that suggests Christ's deity and exalted status. (A similar high Christology can be seen as early as verse 1, where Paul's commission is jointly attributed to Jesus Christ and God the Father.) If grace and peace have their source in the Father God, they equally flow from Jesus Christ, who is God the Son.

Then there is a beautiful statement about Christ's atoning work: He gave Himself for our sins to rescue us from the present evil age. While the Father's role in giving the Son is never to be denied (John 3:16), that is in no way incompatible with the Son's voluntary giving of Himself (10:17-18). Moreover, this self-giving of the Son is in the form of a sacrificial death to atone for our sins. And the purpose of this atonement is to turn us from the sin that surrounds us in this life, though not necessarily to remove us from the world, at least not immediately. Ultimately, of course, the result of Christ's atoning work will be our complete deliverance from evil and the corresponding enjoyment of the age to come.

Furthermore, in an earlier verse (Galatians 1:1) Paul had alluded to Christ's resurrection—also a part of God's redemptive work on our behalf, for in this statement it is the Father who raises the Son. As Paul says elsewhere (Romans 4:25), Christ was raised for our justification. The resurrection of Christ is as much a part of the gospel as is His atoning death.

And all of this rich provision for our salvation had its roots in the will of God in eternity past—"according to the will of our

God and Father" (Galatians 1:4)—and will issue in His glory in the ages to come—"to whom be glory for ever and ever" (1:5).

Such a grand scheme of redemption! And Paul cannot even write the introduction to a letter without these truths coming to the surface. Undoubtedly, this is because they constitute the central teachings of the gospel so dear to Paul's heart.

The gospel is, of course, literally the "good news" about salvation in Jesus Christ. But the good news of the gospel is never completely separated from the bad news concerning the sinful human condition apart from God. That is why Paul says that it is for our *sins* that Christ gave Himself and that it is from this present *evil* age that He rescued us. Unless we accept both this bad news and then the good news that is God's response to the sin of mankind, we have not really understood the full gospel message.

Now there are two ways in which we can fall short of a true comprehension of this negative side of the gospel. One way, which is very typical of us moderns, is simply to deny the reality of human sinfulness. And if we are not sinful, we say, what is the need of salvation and a Savior? This approach denies the gospel by declaring it essentially outmoded, completely unnecessary for autonomous humans, who are the masters of their own fate, the captains of their own souls. And it must be asserted that such an attitude is increasingly common in our own day, in which secularism has convinced many that we are in complete control of our lives and need no interference from any higher being. But in response to this kind of stance, we must unequivocally maintain that there *is* bad news that we need to face squarely, for without it the good news of the gospel is meaningless.

The other way of depreciating the negative side of the gospel message is to feel that we are too sinful to be saved. Here the *bad* news is believed but not the *good* news. While fewer, perhaps, would fit into this mode of thinking, there are some, and they need to be shown the power of the gospel to "rescue us from the present evil age" (1:4)

The prodigal son thought this way at the beginning of his return to his father. At that point he entertained no hope of a full restoration to a position of sonship; he only wanted to be treated as a hired servant, because, he said, "I am no longer worthy to be called your son; make me like one of your hired men" (Luke 15:19). So aware was he of his vile condition that he was unable to hope for a full reinstatement.

On the other hand, some of these who see so clearly their own sinfulness are the very ones who do step out in faith and cast themselves on the mercies of the Savior. The woman "who had lived a sinful life" saw in Jesus one who could help her and brought perfume to anoint His feet (7:37). Thus the bad news about human sinfulness can be overcome through faith.

This theme (the gospel), a concept introduced by Paul right here at the outset of his letter, actually becomes the key to the letter's thought. Almost everything in the letter can be related in some way to this idea of the gospel.

After this epistolary introduction (Galatians 1:1-5), Paul stresses that his gospel, the gospel he proclaimed to the Galatians, is the true gospel, distinct from the perverted message that had been brought to them by false teachers (1:6-10). In the remaining part of chapter 1, he shows the reason that his gospel is the correct one: its origin is ultimately in God. It is not derived from human sources but has its source in God Himself (1:11-24).

In chapter 2 Paul maintains that his gospel, as unique and distinctive as it was, is not incompatible with the form of the gospel proclaimed by those who were apostles from the beginning (2:1-10). Furthermore, when one of those apostles, Peter, engaged in activity that was inconsistent with the gospel that even he believed in and preached, Paul confronted him about this inconsistency. Doing so demonstrated what it meant to carry out the implications of the gospel of grace in a consistent manner (2:11-21).

Then at the heart of the letter to the Galatians Paul comes to the heart of his gospel—the doctrine of salvation by grace through faith. This doctrine is nothing new with Paul; it stands in continuity with God's revelation in the Old Testament (3:1-14). But what then of the law? What was its role, if salvation was always in the economy of God received through faith? In an extended section Paul shows the secondary, temporary nature of the Old Testament ceremonial law. It was never a means of salvation, which was ever by grace through faith, a doctrine with which Paul's gospel is in complete agreement and continuity. Still, the termination in Christ of the ceremonial law entails privileges especially enunciated in Paul's gospel (3:15-4:11).

The tone of the letter shifts as Paul displays a spirit of fervency in calling the Galatians to return to their first loyalty to his gospel. Are they going to settle for a pseudo-gospel that confines them to spiritual bondage and in effect cuts them off from Paul's true gospel of salvation through faith in Christ? Or are they going to reject the false teaching and experience liberty in Christ (4:12-31)?

From this point the emphasis shifts again, now to what ought to be the practical outworking of Paul's gospel. For although Paul firmly *resisted* any doctrine of salvation *by* works, he just as firmly *insisted* that the gospel of salvation by faith must necessarily require good works as a *result* of saving faith. After an initial section laying out a basic perspective on moral behavior (5:1-15), he goes on to show that genuine saving faith will issue in true spirituality—the fruit of the Spirit (5:16-26). It will also necessarily bring forth a life of ministering to others (6:1-10).

Paul concludes this great exposition and defense of his gospel by emphasizing the supreme act of grace that constitutes its foundation—the death of God's own dearly beloved Son on the cross as an atonement for our sins. This unique act is ever for Paul the glory of his gospel (6:11-18).

This in brief is an outline of the book of Galatians. The book really can be analyzed around the theme of Paul's gospel without any sense that the material has been forced into an artificial framework.

While the idea of the gospel is, of course, present whenever the term "gospel" is found, it is also present in other places as well, as in Galatians 1:1-5, which is a brief exposition of the gospel, even though the word itself does not occur.

Clearly the gospel was important to Paul. In fact, although he recognizes it to be the precious possession of the whole church, yet in a special way he considers that God has granted him a unique understanding of it. To this extent, he can think of it not only as the gospel of God or the gospel of Christ, but also as his own gospel. Naturally, this is not to say that Paul is the content of the gospel or the author of the gospel, but that God has given him an especially profound understanding of the gospel of God. True, Paul never uses the actual phrase "my gospel" in the book of Galatians, as he does, for example, in Romans 16:25: "Now to him who is able to establish you by my gospel." On the other hand, the *thought* is clearly present in some passages in the book of Galatians. Consider the following:

- A gospel other than the one we preached (Galatians 1:8)

- The gospel I preached (1:11)

- The gospel that I preach (2:2)

- I had been entrusted with the task of preaching the gospel to the Gentiles (2:7)

With such expressions of Paul's sense of attachment to the gospel, is it any wonder that in the book of Galatians he is defensive of it, ready to challenge even another apostle's understanding of the gospel and its implications? It is entirely in keeping with Paul's statements, then, to use this theme as a framework in which to view the book of Galatians. In fact, such an approach seems to work out rather nicely without any feeling that it is a structure that is alien to the content of the book.

Conclusion

We have chosen to present the book of Galatians according to a perspective that views it as centering in the concept of Paul's gospel. Yet in a far deeper sense, this gospel is God's gospel. It is His because He conceived it, His for accomplishing the redemption that is its foundation, His because it is He who has revealed it to us, and it is His in applying it graciously to our hearts. Little wonder, then, that Paul concludes this opening section with doxology: "To whom be glory for ever and ever."

May it be our response as well. Thanks be to God for His gospel of grace. Praise be to Him for His planning it in eternity past. Glory be to the Revealer-God, who sent His only Son to bring the good news in His person, works and words; who equipped His apostle with skill to understand the good news, with determination to stand firm in that understanding in the face of mighty opponents, and with love and concern for these early believers who struggled in their own attempt to understand the gospel.

Let us thank God Almighty for this gift of the gospel, for its inscripturation in the particular form of the book of Galatians, for its faithful transmission through the ages, for its beacon light in this day of darkness. Let us praise Him for gifts of intelligence He has given us to understand His gospel, for hearts He has opened to receive its teachings, for the blessed privilege of proclaiming it across the street and around the world, and for each opportunity to be exposed again and again to its power and majesty. "To Him be glory for ever and ever. Amen."

O what amazing words of grace are in the gospel
  found,
Suited to every sinner's case who knows the joyful
  sound.
Poor, sinful, thirsty, fainting souls are freely
  welcome here.
Salvation, like a river, rolls abundant, free, and
  clear.[9]

Questions for Reflection or Discussion

1. Who are the brothers Paul refers to in Galatians 1:2? What are the implications of his calling them brothers?

2. What are the implications of Christ's rescuing us from the present evil age?

3. What does it mean for glory to be to God for ever and ever?

4. Jesus is distinguished from God in verses 1 and 3. How should we respond to someone who claims that Jesus is not God because of this distinction?

Endnotes

1. Romans 16, for example, offers abundant cases of Paul sending greetings to individual Roman Christians (16:3-16) and greetings from people who were with him at the time of writing (16:21-24).

2. J.B. Lightfoot, *Saint Paul's Epistle to the Galatians* (London: MacMillan and Co., 1921), 227.

3. In Ignatius' letter to the Magnesians 8:1: "for if we live according to Judaism, we confess that we have not received grace" seems to reflect Galatians 5:4, while in Polycarp's letter to the Philippians 5:1: "God is not mocked" echoes Galatians 6:7. Furthermore, his reference to the faith in 3:2 as the mother of us all seems to be based on Galatians 4:26.

4. Paul Feine and Johannes Behm, *Introduction to the New Testament*, ed. W.G. Kuemmel, trans. A.J. Mattill, Jr. (Nashville: Abingdon Press, 1966), 178.

5. Actually, it is not clear that there even was an evangelizing of the northern area by Paul. True, Acts 16:6 states that "Paul and his companions traveled throughout the region of Phrygia and Galatia," and Acts 18:23 refers to disciples in that area, but even in these passages the precise identification of the key term is not entirely clear.

6. Very much involved in this whole question of the date of the epistle is how one relates the two visits to Jerusalem Paul mentions in Galatians (1:18-24; 2:1-10) to the several early visits of Paul recorded in the book of Acts (9:26-30; 11:30; 15:2-29). Specifically, much depends on whether Galatians 2:1-10 is identified with the "famine visit" of Acts 11:30 or the Jerusalem Council visit of Acts 15. A recent statement of the case for the former view is given in Leon Morris, *Galatians: Paul's Charter of Christian Freedom* (Downers Grove: InterVarsity Press, 1996), 20-22.

7. Moises Silva, *Explorations in Exegetical Method: Galatians as a Test Case* (Grand Rapids: Baker Books, 1996), 129-139.

8. I do not find the need to be more precise about the historical setting of the book to be pressing. It would be nice to be able to be more specific, but I am not convinced that the general interpretation of specific passages would be materially different, given another set of circumstances than the one adopted. The most important consideration is that these were Paul's personal converts.

9. Samuel Medley, "O What Amazing Words of Grace Are in the Gospel Found" (a hymn).

2

The Correctness of Paul's Gospel

Galatians 1:6-10

I am astonished that you are so quickly deserting the one who called you by the grace of Christ and are turning to a different gospel—which is really no gospel at all. Evidently some people are throwing you into confusion and are trying to pervert the gospel of Christ. But even if we or an angel from heaven should preach a gospel other than the one we preached to you, let him be eternally condemned! As we have already said, so now I say again: If anybody is preaching to you a gospel other than what you accepted, let him be eternally condemned!

Am I now trying to win the approval of men, or of God? Or am I trying to please men? If I were still trying to please men, I would not be a servant of Christ.

There is an interesting story, popular in an earlier era but little read nowadays, entitled *The Cloister and the Hearth.* The tale is set in fifteenth-century Holland and is about a young couple, Gerard and Margaret. They were devotedly in love with each other, but their prospective marriage was unfairly opposed by the young man's family. However, rather than give her up, he fled his native land in order to earn money in Italy as an artist and then return to claim his beloved.

After a long delay, in which both remained faithful in their love, the young woman wrote imploring her fiancé to return and entrusted the letter to a friend. But Gerard's enemies intercepted the courier and substituted another letter, which said that Margaret had died and that Gerard should not bother to return.

One cannot begin to imagine the tragic impact this had on the young man when he received the letter. He received the wrong message, and his reaction to that false message had tragic and irreversible consequences. So discouraged was he that from his purposeful life of industry and accomplishment, he plunged himself into debauchery and dissolution, eventually coming to the point of attempting suicide.

Miraculously, he was rescued by a friend and handed over for recovery into the care of a convent, where his faith was gradually restored and he dedicated himself to the priesthood of the church and a life of celibacy. Excelling in his calling, Gerard was appointed to preaching ministry in his homeland, where he came to realize the dastardly plot that had been carried out against him. But now, although comforted by the fact that Margaret was still alive, he could not be fully united with her as man with wife. And thus they were forced to live out their lives in daily association, but he in the service of the cloister and she in the common life of the hearth.

But as heartrending as our response to this fictional human situation might be, how much more should be our concern when it is the message of eternal salvation at stake. And it was precisely that gospel of eternal salvation that Paul considered to be at stake in the Galatian situation. If there is anything certain in Galatians studies, it is that Paul was unalterably committed to the understanding of the gospel he believed God had entrusted to him: his gospel. Other emphases in the early Church concerning God's redemptive work may legitimately have existed—for example, the emphasis on the proclamation of the gospel to Jewish audiences, an emphasis held by Paul's apostolic colleagues in Jerusalem. But he had limits, in his mind, to the deviation from his gospel that he could tolerate. Certainly any interpretation of the gospel that exceeded those limits was, as Paul expresses it in 1:7, a perversion of the gospel.

It is this issue concerning the perversion of the gospel that opens the discussion in this letter to the Galatians. Consequently, we will look at the kinds of perversion, the causes of this particular perversion being encountered in the Galatian context, and the consequences of perverting the gospel.

Kinds of Perversion

Paul does not actually analyze the different kinds of perversion here in this section. Nevertheless, we can see from what he does say elsewhere in the epistle and from Scripture generally that there are essentially two ways of perverting the gospel of Christ: either by adding extraneous elements to it or by deleting one or more elements from it. The former perversion, that of addition to the gospel, we may call the legalist perversion; the term "libertine perversion" seems an apt way of describing the perversion by deletion.

Legalist perversion

It was the legalist perversion that occupied most of Paul's attention in this letter. Apparently, those who were troubling the Galatian believers were intent on requiring them to adhere to certain aspects of the Old Testament ceremonial law, particularly the requirement of circumcision (5:3). In addition to that practice, other elements of the ceremonial law also appear to have been stressed as well. Thus there seems to have been a concern that the Gentile converts observe certain holy days required in Old Testament law (4:9), and it is plausible that attention may also have been devoted to elements of the Jewish customs surrounding the Old Testament food laws.[1]

Paul viewed these emphases of the false teachers as unnecessary additions to the gospel for the Gentiles, essentially threatening the gospel of grace. In fact, he no doubt saw them as likewise unnecessary for Jewish believers, unnecessary at least from a theological perspective. It is one thing for Jewish believers to engage in their traditional rituals, but it is quite another for them to do so out of a sense of necessity as believers in Christ. Indeed, Paul may not ultimately have objected even to Gentile believers engaging in these practices as long as they were not interpreted as additional requirements for salvation or Christian living. But the line between engaging in them for oneself as voluntary adherence to traditional customs and insisting on them for others as standards of Christian behavior is a fine one, and Paul seems to have been extremely zealous to guard that boundary carefully.

This legalist way of perverting the message of God was nothing new. Our Lord Himself faced the same general phenomenon when he confronted the traditions of the scribes. In a well-known controversy with them Jesus said, "You have a fine way of setting aside the commands of God in order to observe your own traditions" (Mark 7:9; see also Matthew 15:3, 6). True, this particular example from the ministry of Christ is not a perversion of the *gospel,* but the principle of perverting the word of God by adding elements to it is the same. Moreover, it can be seen in this example that in a very real sense the legalist perversion of the gospel is not merely adding to the gospel. Rather, in adding elements to the gospel, it is actually overthrowing it.

Likewise, the legalist perversion of the gospel is by no means a thing of the past; it is very possible that emphases in the modern theological scene that require adherence to certain practices or lifestyle standards fall into the same basic category. For example, there comes to mind the insistence there might be in some quarters on a particular form of baptism or on a rebaptism performed by what would be considered an authentic officiant. As important as the rite of baptism is biblically, one may wonder whether sometimes it becomes in some of our traditions an addition to the pure gospel itself. All of this is not to say, of course, that certain lifestyle issues are unimportant, for undoubtedly they are. But there is something wrong when they become so enmeshed with the message of salvation that the pure gospel message is distorted.

Libertine perversion

Paul's attention to the libertine perversion of the gospel is far less extensive in this letter than is his interest in the legalist perversion, but an intimation of his deep concern can be observed in Galatians 5:13. There he warns against a concept of freedom that essentially eliminates an important aspect of the gospel: "You, my brothers, were called to be free. But do not use your freedom to indulge the sinful nature." To preach that kind of gospel is to preach a perversion.

Once again, it must be observed that certain forms of the libertine perversion are with us today in any proclamation of the gospel that fails to do justice to its ethical implications. There exists a wide variety of shades in this tendency, all the way from a clear antinomianism, to so-called situational ethics, to statements of the gospel at the conservative end of the theological spectrum that put forth a message of salvation without a truly biblical concept of repentance. But whatever its form, the elimination of a significant element of the gospel is finally an insidious perversion of its message.

The attempt to combine a full-fledged antinomianism with the Christian message was by no means absent from the ancient world either. Some Gnostic thinkers tried to combine Christian themes with a Greek-like disparagement of the body whereby things done in the body were deemed morally neutral and thus of no moral consequence. Perhaps technically this system of thought cannot be said to be absolutely without a principle of law, but at least it is without law in the sense of its having no interest in the traditional concerns of law.

Such an antinomian tendency as this, while it may not be as fully developed as in the Gnostic system briefly described above, seems also to be present already in the century of the New Testament's composition, as the twin epistles of Second Peter and Jude attest. Peter, referring to false teachers among the Christian communities of his readers, generally mentions their shameful ways (2 Peter 2:1-2). The parallel passage in Jude is more explicit, saying, "Certain men . . . have secretly slipped in among you. They are godless men, who change the grace of our God into a license for immorality" (Jude 4). And again Jude charges, "These dreamers pollute their own bodies" (8). So even if this antinomian thinking was not present at Galatia to the extent that the legalist perversion of the gospel was found there, it was a reality the apostolic community in general had to contend with.

In modern times, situation ethics, at least in its most respectable form, does not dispense with the principle of law entirely. Rather, it insists that there is only one law—the law of love for one's neighbor—to which all other ethical principles must yield.

But what this form of the gospel leaves out is the other great ethical principle enunciated by our Lord—loving the Lord God with all the heart, soul, mind and strength. Not only is this a second principle, but it is a higher principle; it is the first commandment, to which the law of neighbor love takes second place.

Of course, the response of situation ethics is that the two commands are reducible to one: loving God is loving one's neighbor, and loving one's neighbor is loving God. But such a response hardly deals adequately with the terminology of a "first commandment" and a "second commandment."

Another version of a truncated gospel is the attempt today on the part of some evangelical teachers to interpret the gospel in terms of a salvation bestowed through our trusting in Christ's atoning work but not necessarily involving, at the point of conversion, an attitude of repentance, in the sense of a turning from sin. Rather, repentance is seen merely as a change of attitude toward the human condition and the nature of Christ. According to this interpretation of the gospel, if we have thought of human nature as essentially good, we must change our mind and adopt God's attitude regarding human sinfulness in general and about our involvement in it. If we have considered Christ as simply a great human being, we need to change our mind and see Him as truly God. But, according to this view, any thought of repentance as a turning from sin is not to be considered as essential for accepting Christ as a personal Savior.[2]

In this version of the gospel something very important has been omitted. It may be somewhat unfair to call this kind of thinking libertine, but at least it shares with the obviously libertine versions of the gospel a willingness to remove an essential element (turning from sin) from the gospel message.[3]

So we have, then, both in the New Testament times and in modern theologies the legalist and libertine perversions of the gospel. It is intriguing that the two forms of perversion, the legalist and the libertine, while seemingly at opposite ends of a spectrum, may not be entirely incompatible. That is, one could both add to the gospel in some areas and at the same time remove some of the basic elements from it; one could be both legalist and libertine. But whether we succumb to one or the other or both of these errors, we are on dangerous ground.

Causes of Perversion

The factors that brought the false intruders to pervert the gospel in the way they did were both internal and external.

Internally, the perversion came from their own will; they *wanted* to pervert it, says Paul (Galatians 1:7). Actually, the common translation given in the NIV is a little misleading, for the word translated "trying" in this version is a word that more commonly means "wanting."[4] Paul represents the false teachers as desiring to pervert the gospel message, although there is no further probing here regarding their motive for doing so.

On the other hand, the temptation to distort the gospel may also derive from a desire to respond to external forces, that is, in this particular case, to win the approval of others: "to please men" (1:10).

Actually, these two factors are intimately related: the will does not operate purely internally; its desires are in response to factors external to it. Nevertheless, at least in this particular case, the will is involved; the behavior cannot be attributed to the external factors alone.

This is not to say, of course, that there cannot be distortion of the gospel unless someone consciously wills to distort it. Surely there is the possibility of distortion through ignorance. We naturally think of those about whom Christ speaks in Matthew 7:21-23, who claimed to have prophesied in Christ's name. Are we not to think that their claim was sincere, albeit misguided?

Or take the case of the prophet Hananiah in the days of Jeremiah (Jeremiah 28). Is it clear that his erroneous message concerning the relatively brief length of Judah's captivity in Babylon was motivated by malice, or political pressure, or material gain? Not necessarily. His representation of the word of God was indeed incorrect, but it was probably given in all sincerity and good faith and in the conviction that he was in the right.

But that is not the case with Paul's opponents at Galatia, as he makes abundantly clear in the passage before us. Their perversion of the gospel was in his view deliberate; they willfully distorted it. Their reasons are probably now no longer recoverable, but that it was intentional can hardly be in doubt. In this regard, they were like the false teachers confronted by Jude, when he says of them, "They follow their own evil desires; they boast about themselves and flatter others for their own advantage" (Jude 16).

On the other hand, it is curious that the proclamation of the gospel may actually escape perversion, even when less-than-pure motives are involved. We think, in this regard, of Paul's statement to the Philippians (1:15, 17-18):

> It is true that some preach Christ out of envy and rivalry, but others out of goodwill. . . . The former preach Christ out of selfish ambition, not sincerely, supposing that they can stir up trouble for me while I am in chains. But what does it matter? The important thing is that in every way, whether from false motives or true, Christ is preached.

Strangely, God could use the preaching of His Word, even though the ones proclaiming it might have operated from rather peculiar motives.

Whatever the factors involved in the particular instance pertaining to the Galatians, Paul's alluding to the possible causes of perversion gives us reason to ponder our own motives, lest they should somehow lead to our distorting the truth of Christ's message.

At the same time, these reflections by Paul on the need for pleasing God rather than men present to us one of the many ways of viewing the "deeper life." There can hardly be any perspective deeper than the thought of focusing our lives in a

Godward direction, seeking to please Him in all we say and do and even think. Let us, like Paul, endeavor to be God-pleasers.

Consequences of Perversion

There are severe consequences attached to those who would preach a distorted gospel. Paul has only harsh warnings to give concerning them. "But even if we or an angel from heaven should preach a gospel other than the one we preached to you, let him be eternally condemned!" (Galatians 1:8). There could certainly not be a more dreaded fate than the eternal destruction he wishes for those who pervert the gospel. Paul is so emphatic on this point that he says virtually the same thing again in verse 9!

But if Paul can use stern warnings against those who would *preach* a perversion of the gospel, he likewise warns those who *hear and entertain* such perversions. One consequence of listening and giving heed to a perverted gospel is that it brings only trouble, disturbance and confusion. This is a far cry from the peace that comes from the true gospel message (1:3). This confusion, if left unchecked, could lead to the severest of consequences, ultimately to turning from the gospel and from Christ and His grace ("deserting the one who called you," 1:6).

And yet herein lies what must surely be one of the most difficult problems of the book of Galatians. Paul seems to be saying that one can actually turn from God's efficacious calling. How can this be? How can anything effectual be overturned?

First, we note that the Galatians are in danger of turning not just from Paul's invitation to receive the gospel, but from *God's* calling. Further, it is an efficacious call, one that effectively brings about salvation in Christ, as is Paul's customary meaning for the term "call."[5] These observations leave us essentially with the unresolved paradox of turning from a work of God that supposedly has assured results. How should we understand this paradox?

One way of dealing with this difficulty would be simply to note it, leave it unresolved and go on. Others might want to see in this verse evidence that a believer can actually turn from effective calling and lose salvation. But, of course, the verse hardly says this, and in any case it would not relieve the logical tension to talk about losing that which has been efficaciously wrought.

A better solution would be to say that Paul is using the language of appearance, that the turning from efficacious calling is not actual but simply the way things appear to be. If the calling really did produce salvation, then their "turning" only appeared to be a turning from the gospel. On the other hand, if there really was a turning from the gospel, then there was no truly effectual calling at work in their lives to begin with. They may have been given the gospel invitation and may even have responded in some way to it, but genuine effectual calling by God was not present in their experience.

With these considerations in mind, we may conclude that Paul's purpose may well have been to use such shockingly paradoxical language in order to arouse the Galatians to turn once again, this time from the path they seem to have chosen, back to the truth of God's gospel.

Conclusion

Whatever we may conclude about this difficult text, there is no doubt whatsoever about Paul's concern that the gospel not be perverted. If the gospel which is proclaimed is not the correct gospel, the pure gospel, it is no gospel at all. It is not the good news, but some other thing disguised as the good news. What a tragedy if this is the "gospel" that people hear from our pulpits or in our attempts to engage people evangelistically!

What unfortunate consequences will result from people hearing the wrong message!

Giving and receiving the wrong message were not new phenomena in Paul's day. Throughout the Old Testament one finds the true message being confronted by the false, and it was not always easy for the hearer to distinguish between them. But just as Paul could sense that the message of the Judaizers was essentially false, so could the true prophet in the Old Testament have the awareness, at least on occasion, that the competing message was in error. Hear the cry of Jeremiah (23:16-18).

> Do not listen to what the prophets are prophesying to
> you;
> they fill you with false hopes.
> They speak visions from their own minds,
> not from the mouth of the LORD.
> They keep saying to those who despise me,
> "The LORD says . . ."
> But which of them has stood in the council of the
> LORD
> to see or to hear his word?

So Jeremiah knew himself to be God's spokesman and in competition with other prophets whose message was false.

Nor did the problem end with Paul and the Judaizers. John is equally clear in his first epistle that there is a distinct difference between the message of truth and the message of error (1 John 4:5-6):

> They are from the world and therefore speak from the
> viewpoint of the world, and the world listens to them.
> We are from God, and whoever knows God listens to
> us; but whoever is not from God does not listen to us.
> This is how we recognize the Spirit of truth and the
> spirit of falsehood.

Paul's gospel is the correct gospel. Let us make every effort to proclaim the correct gospel and not some perversion of it. To borrow once again from the book of Jude, let us "contend for the faith that was once for all entrusted to the saints" (Jude 3). But if it is a shameful thing to proclaim a false gospel, it is equally reprehensible to choose to listen to one. Paul's words to Timothy are appropriate here: "For the time will come when men will not put up with sound doctrine. Instead, to suit their own desires, they will gather around them a great number of teachers to say what their itching ears want to hear" (2 Timothy 4:3). May we never be guilty of listening to a message claiming to be the gospel of Christ, but in fact being only a perversion thereof.

Lord, speak to me, that I may speak
   in living echoes of Thy tone;
As Thou hast sought, so let me seek
   Thy erring children, lost and lone.
Oh, lead me, Lord, that I may lead
   the wandering and the wavering feet;
Oh, feed me, Lord, that I may feed
   Thy hungering ones with manna sweet.
Oh, strengthen me, that while I stand
   firm on the rock and strong in Thee,
I may stretch out a loving hand
   to wrestlers with the troubled sea.
Oh, teach me, Lord, that I may teach
   the precious things Thou dost impart;
And wing my words, that they may reach
   the hidden depths of many a heart.
Oh, fill me with Thy fullness, Lord,
   until my very heart o'erflow
In kindling thought and glowing word,

Thy love to tell, Thy praise to show.
Oh, use me, Lord, use even me,
   just as Thou wilt, and when, and where,
Until Thy blessed face I see,
   Thy rest, Thy joy, Thy glory share.[6]

Questions for Reflection or Discussion

1. Why is Paul so astonished in Galatians 1:6?
2. What is meant by deserting? Is it total or partial?
3. What does Paul mean by the grace *of Christ* (1:6)?
4. Is there any distinction between being called in the grace of Christ (RSV) and being called by the grace of Christ (NIV)?
5. In verse 6 Paul uses the word "desert" (meta*tithesthe*), and in verse 7 the word "pervert" (meta*strepsai*), both words being compounds with meta-. Do you think there is a connection? If so, what?
6. What does Second Thessalonians 1:9 reveal about Paul's concept of eternal condemnation (Galatians 1:8)?
7. What does the word "still" imply (1:10)?

Endnotes

1. At any rate, such is clearly the case in the generally parallel Colossians 2:16.
2. A responsible statement of this position may be found in Charles C. Ryrie, *So Great Salvation* (Wheaton: Scripture Press Publications, Inc., 1989).
3. Note the following passages where turning from sin is viewed as part of the gospel proclamation (emphases mine): Acts 3:26, "When God raised up his servant, he sent him first to you to bless you *by turning each of you from your wicked ways*"; Acts 26:20, "I preached that they should repent and turn to God *and prove their repentance by their deeds.*"

4. The Greek word is *thelontes.* The NIV's "trying" is not wrong; it is just not as explicit as it could be.
5. Undoubtedly the clearest Pauline example of calling being efficacious is Romans 8:30, "Those he called . . . he also glorified."
6. Frances R. Havergal, "A Worker's Prayer," *Hymns of the Christian Life* (Camp Hill, PA: Christian Publications, 1978), # 373.

3

The Origin of Paul's Gospel

Galatians 1:11-24

I want you to know, brothers, that the gospel I preached is not something that man made up. I did not receive it from any man, nor was I taught it; rather, I received it by revelation from Jesus Christ.

For you have heard of my previous way of life in Judaism, how intensely I persecuted the church of God and tried to destroy it. I was advancing in Judaism beyond many Jews of my own age and was extremely zealous for the traditions of my fathers. But when God, who set me apart from birth and called me by his grace, was pleased to reveal his Son in me so that I might preach him among the Gentiles, I did not consult any man, nor did I go up to Jerusalem to see those who were apostles before I was, but I went immediately into Arabia and later returned to Damascus.

Then after three years, I went up to Jerusalem to get acquainted with Peter and stayed with him fifteen days. I saw none of the other apostles—only James, the Lord's brother. I assure you before God that what I am writing you is no lie. Later I went to Syria and Cilicia. I was personally unknown to the churches of Judea that are in Christ. They only heard the report: "The man who formerly persecuted us is now preaching the faith he once tried to destroy." And they praised God because of me.

S ome years ago, a well-known brokerage firm came out with the slogan, "When E.F. Hutton talks, people listen." It is no longer the case that people in general listen when *God* speaks. But that state of affairs was not always so.

In the days of Elijah, a humble widow could discern the voice of God in the ministry of His prophet. Earlier, in her poverty, she had supported the fugitive man of God and had witnessed the miracle of her jug of oil never running dry. But when her only son became sick and died, she blamed Elijah, who in the boldness of faith placed the matter in the Lord's hands. God answered the prophet's prayer and restored the boy to life, at which point the unnamed woman uttered these profound words: "Now I know that you are a man of God and that the word of the LORD from your mouth is the truth" (1 Kings 17:24). If Elijah spoke from God, the word was true.

Such is the case also with Paul. His gospel is from God. We have already seen how Paul, sensing the urgency of the Galatians' situation and expressing his concern for them, nevertheless insists that his gospel is the correct gospel and that the Galatians should not listen to the pseudo-gospel being presented to them. He now proceeds to give the Galatians the reason why his gospel is the only true gospel: his had its origin in God. It did not have its derivation from his own experience or from any other human authority but came from God Himself.

Paul's confident assertion about the divine origin of his gospel has in itself decisive value in proving the correctness of Paul's gospel, for if it comes from God, how can it be less than correct? So one of Paul's motives in stressing this consideration is to underscore points he had already made: his gospel speaks truth.

It is also possible that the false teachers who were causing problems among the Galatians had made an issue of Paul not being an original disciple of Jesus and therefore not qualified to claim any uniqueness or correctness relating to his message. So to some extent Paul's remarks here may be a response to these accusations, attempting to lay out exactly what his relations with the original apostles were. In any case, his discussion takes an autobiographical turn, highlighting certain critical moments in his career in order to show that his gospel came from God and not from any other source.

The claim of divine origin is supported by three lines of argumentation: 1) Paul's gospel cannot be explained in any other way than that it was of divine origin; 2) it was revealed to him directly by God through His Son; and 3) the fact of its being independent of human origin was confirmed by its reception by the people of God.

Unexplained by Alternative Causes

Paul begins by asserting that no explanation can be given for his gospel except that it is of divine origin. There is nothing in his religious background that can explain it, nor is it explainable in terms of its being derived from those who were leaders in the church before his conversion.

Not from ancestral upbringing (1:11-14)

In showing that his gospel does not come from any human origin, Paul first points out that it could not have come from anything in his ancestral background. Although he had received a strict religious training in Judaism, this alone could not even begin to account for the way his gospel developed.

There were, of course, many similarities between the Judaism of Paul's upbringing and some of the tenets of his gospel. After all, such cardinal doctrines as the being and attributes of God, His creation of the world and His providential care of its creatures, the hope in redemption and the resurrection—all these and more would represent a strong thread of continuity between Paul's earlier Pharisaism and his newfound Christian thinking.

Furthermore, our own experience tells us that upbringing does exert a shaping influence on our behavior—shaping, but not necessarily determinative. For that matter, heredity also has its hand in how we develop and consequently how we come to act and even believe. But as strong as these influences may be in our lives, they can to some extent be resisted and overcome. People do change; they do convert from one point of view to another in such a manner that the new mode of thinking is simply not attributable to their origins.

So it was with Paul. In spite of the many common points of outlook he shared with his upbringing, some of Paul's previous religious experience had been almost diametrically opposed to some key elements in the gospel he later proclaimed. Thus there is no reasonable way that the former could be in any meaningful sense the source of the latter.

Not only had he been deeply involved in Judaism's attitudes toward the Law of Moses, but he had also been fully devoted to persecuting and destroying the new developments found in the Christian gospel. Listen to his own testimony to this effect when he addressed the multitudes in Jerusalem at the time of his arrest:

> I am a Jew, born in Tarsus of Cilicia, but brought up in this city. Under Gamaliel I was thoroughly trained in the law of our fathers and was just as zealous for God as any of you are today. I persecuted the followers of this Way to their death, arresting both men and women and throwing them into prison. (Acts 22:3-4)

Or again, before Festus and King Agrippa,

The Jews all know the way I have lived ever since I was a child, from the beginning of my life in my own country, and also in Jerusalem. They have known me for a long time and can testify, if they are willing, that according to the strictest sect of our religion, I lived as a Pharisee. (26:4-5)

And, of course, what Paul claimed in these statements recorded by Luke in the second volume of his early Christian history is now reaffirmed here in Galatians 1:13-14, when the apostle states: "For you have heard of my previous way of life in Judaism, how intensely I persecuted the church of God and tried to destroy it. I was advancing in Judaism beyond many Jews of my own age and was extremely zealous for the traditions of my fathers."

In the light of these statements, it is therefore unthinkable that the Pauline gospel is simply an application of Jewish teaching to a new situation. It did not come simply from his ancestral upbringing.

Not from the Jerusalem apostles (1:17-21)

On the other hand, if Paul's gospel does not derive from the human authority of his ancestry, neither does it spring from the human authority of the apostles who were the original appointees of Christ Himself.

This is primarily due to the fact that Paul's contact with the Jerusalem apostles was minimal. He stresses that he did not, upon his conversion, travel to Jerusalem to meet with them and consult with them. Rather, he went into relative seclusion—to "Arabia"—although he does not fill in explicitly his purpose in retiring there. It may have been intentionally to avoid contact with the Jerusalem apostles so that he could "hammer out" his distinctive theology on his own with God. In any event, he was not in their presence, and therefore was not beholden to them for his theological outlook.

Then, when he did have contact with them, it took place only after this rather extended period of three years of independent development. Whether he intended it or not, this relative privacy had the effect of giving him abundant opportunity to develop, under God, his own unique insight into the implications of the gospel for Gentile believers.

Furthermore, the contact with the Jewish Christian leaders in Jerusalem was limited to Peter and James, the brother of Jesus, and even then the contact was not extended, but only lasted a couple of weeks. Then Paul left them to go to Syria and Cilicia. Surely this would indicate that the apostle's basic theological outlook had already been formulated and that he owed little to those who were apostles before he became one.

Of these facts and their relevance Paul is so confident that he is willing, in effect, to take a solemn oath before God to their truth and accuracy: "I assure you before God that what I am writing you is no lie" (1:20).

Thus by rehearsing this historical data, Paul was supporting his contention that his gospel was of *divine* origin. It cannot be explained otherwise. His gospel was neither from his ancestral background nor from contacts with the apostolic band. It was from God, not man.

Revealed by God (1:15-16)

But not only could Paul argue the point negatively—that is, by claiming that his gospel was not of human origin—but his claim was also, positively, that it was from God. Here we see Paul making his point in several different ways.

First, he was, like the prophet Jeremiah, set apart from birth for his Christian ministry as well as called to it (1:15). It may have taken a long time for Paul to come to this realization, but

eventually he would come to understand it quite clearly. God
had his hand in Paul's development from the very beginning of
his life, although much of his earlier life was diverted into behavior that was not fully pleasing to God. Nevertheless, God
was providentially in charge.

Furthermore, it was God's will, purpose and good pleasure
to come to Paul in a special and direct revelation—"to reveal
his Son in me so that I might preach him among the Gentiles"
(1:16)—certainly a reference to the resurrected Christ's appearance to him on the road to Damascus when he said, "I am
Jesus, whom you are persecuting" (Acts 9:5; 22:8), and Saul
the Jew became Saul the Christian believer.

This crucial event was clearly central to Paul and to his
self-awareness of apostleship. From the outset, whether Paul
himself understood it completely or not, the encounter with the
risen Christ had as its goal his peculiar ministry to the Gentile
world and also, therefore, his insight into the nature of Gentile
conversion—that is, his gospel. Indeed, when he recounted the
event of his conversion before Herod Agrippa, the great apostle
made this commission from Christ explicit, representing Him
as saying:

> I have appeared to you to appoint you as a servant and
> as a witness of what you have seen of me and what I
> will show you. I will rescue you from your own people
> and from the Gentiles. I am sending you to them to
> open their eyes and turn them from darkness to light,
> and from the power of Satan to God, so that they may
> receive forgiveness of sins and a place among those
> who are sanctified by faith in me. (Acts 26:16-18)

We may not share with Paul such a dramatic encounter nor
see the vision he saw. Yet the sense of personally hearing the
message of God through His Word is the precious possession of
every believer, giving us the conviction that we too have truths

that are of divine origin. This is not to say, of course, that we have truths that conflict with Scripture or even ones that supplement that inspired revelation, but only truth that is implied in Scripture and is brought to light in our minds by the Spirit of God. Thus we may say with the hymnist:

> I ask no dream, no prophet ecstasies,
>   no sudden rending of the veil of clay,
> No angel visitant, no opening skies;
>   but take the dimness of my soul away.[1]

Confirmed by God's People (Galatians 1:22-24)

Furthermore, as conclusive as this evidence is in supporting Paul's claim to the divine origin of his gospel, there is yet another factor that supports his claim, and that is the ready acceptance Paul received from the churches of Judea. Certainly these early Christian believers throughout Judea saw nothing deficient about Paul's gospel, nothing that was not orthodox, nothing that suggested he was corrupting the early gospel proclamation by adding to it or detracting from it. To the contrary, they received the favorable reports about his conversion and his preaching and gave praise to God for it. Where others might have been skeptical or suspicious of the genuineness of Paul's conversion and calling to preach the gospel of Christ, these noble believers, ordinary folk though they were, did not hesitate to accept him as a brother and fellow-proclaimer of the true faith.

These people Paul is talking about are probably best thought of as Christians scattered throughout the countryside of Judea, rather than believers in the immediate environs of Jerusalem itself, where Paul presumably would have been known through his presence there as a prominent young and zealous Jewish leader.

There are no better illustrations of this willingness to accept a new convert than the examples of Ananias and Barnabas. The actions of these brothers in Christ would be especially meaningful to Paul, as he was the recipient of their cordiality. Ananias, it will be recalled, at first resisted his God-given responsibility to receive Saul into the family of believers, but then, charged by the Lord to "Go," he went to welcome him, and the first words out of his mouth at their meeting were the welcoming words, "Brother Saul" (Acts 9:10-17).

Then later, we see the same attitude of receptivity in the welcome of Saul by Barnabas, for we read, "When he came to Jerusalem, he tried to join the disciples, but they were all afraid of him, not believing that he really was a disciple. But Barnabas took him" (9:26-27).

It is important that Christians, and especially Christian leaders, be acknowledged by the established people of God. Perhaps even more to the point is the kind of recognition of gifts and calling to ministry that the people of God display when they ordain a person to Christian service. A person may legitimately feel called to ministry, but unless that calling is recognized and ratified, so to speak, by the people of God, it remains incomplete and very likely not fully effectual. Once again it is the body of ordinary believers that is used of God to authenticate the role of a Christian leader.

Conclusion

Paul's claim to speak the word of God is indeed a bold one. But it does not stand alone in the history of divine revelation. We are reminded of the foundational passage containing the law of the prophet in Deuteronomy (18:18-19), where the Lord says: "I will put my words in his mouth, and he will tell them everything I command him. If anyone does not listen to my words that the prophet speaks in my name, I myself will call him to account."

This claim to speak the very words of God is echoed again and again throughout the Scriptures by many prophets. Ezekiel was but one of these, when he claimed that the Lord had charged him: "You must speak my words to them, whether they listen or fail to listen. . . . Listen to what I say to you. . . . Open your mouth and eat what I give you" (Ezekiel 2:7-8).

Thus, Paul was, as it were, a prophet of God, receiving direct revelation from the Almighty. His words, therefore, must be heeded; his gospel must be believed and obeyed.

There is, of course, another sense in which the validity of a message is determined not only by its origins but also by its results. Recall the wise counsel of Gamaliel, in which the determination of whether the message of the followers of Jesus was from God or not depended to some extent on its ultimate results. Referring to the apostles' attempts to witness before the Jewish nation, Gamaliel advised his compatriots, "If their purpose or activity is of human origin, it will fail. But if it is from God, you will not be able to stop these men; you will only find yourselves fighting against God" (Acts 5:38-39). We might even see an echo of his words in Paul's argument in this first chapter of Galatians. Even Christ Himself taught that same principle: "By their fruit you will recognize them" (Matthew 7:20).

If the gospel of Paul is the gospel of God, the message preached by Paul's opponents cannot be. Only one of them is the true gospel, and its truth is guaranteed by its divine origin.

This discussion of the origin of Paul's gospel is not merely a theoretical academic exercise. It has far-reaching practical application as well. How willing are we to receive those new to the faith? Do we reach out to new converts so as to add strength to their sense of belonging to the people of God? Do we allow ourselves to be God's instruments to affirm a new believer in the faith? Surely we can benefit from seeing this marvelous example of Christian welcome that we have here in Paul's recounting of his own acceptance by the Judean Christians.

Once again, how grounded in the gospel are we ourselves? Are we able to evaluate effectively the message of those claiming to preach and teach the gospel of Christ? Can we separate the chaff from the pure wheat of the gospel and discern the true message of God in the midst of the many conflicting voices surrounding us?

Applying the teaching of this passage in a different direction, we note again Paul's experience of personal communion with God, for there was undoubtedly a good bit of that taking place during his sojourn in Arabia. And if such a sense of intimate communion with God was appropriate for the great apostle, surely it is relevant to us in our attempt to pursue the deeper life. How would our lives and ministries be affected by times of intimacy with our Redeemer?

Naturally, the concept of intimacy can be abused. We do not advocate an overly familiar attitude toward the Almighty, one in which we presume upon His holiness and grace. But a relationship of reverent intimacy with God is both what He desires of us and what will benefit us as well. "The chief end of man is to glorify God and to *enjoy* Him forever," says the Westminster Catechism.

Nor is such intimacy to be thought of as reserved for a spiritual or intellectual elite. It is available to anyone who will make the effort toward the pursuit of God. As Paul says to the Corinthians:

> Not many of you were wise by human standards; not many were influential; not many were of noble birth. But God chose the foolish things of the world to shame the wise; God chose the weak things of the world to shame the strong. He chose the lowly things

of this world and the despised things—and the things that are not—to nullify the things that are, so that no one may boast before him. It is because of him that you are in Christ Jesus, who has become for us wisdom from God—that is, our righteousness, holiness and redemption. (1 Corinthians 1:26-30)

Wisdom from God: that is what Paul claims regarding his gospel. Let us accept that claim and embrace that gospel with our whole being.

Almighty Lord, the sun shall fail,
    the moon forget her nightly tale,
and deepest silence hush on high
    the radiant chorus of the sky.
But fixed for everlasting years,
    unmoved amid the wreck of spheres,
Thy word shall shine in cloudless day,
    when heaven and earth have passed away.[2]

Questions for Reflection or Discussion

1. What is implied in Paul's use of the word "brothers" (Galatians 1:11)?
2. Why did Paul refer to the church as "the church of God" (1:13)?
3. Is there special significance of "in" in the phrase "reveal his Son in me" (1:16)?
4. What does Paul mean by "Arabia" (1:17)?
5. What is implied in "get acquainted" (1:18)?
6. Is James called an apostle in 1:19? If so, what are the implications of that fact?
7. Why would Paul use the plural "churches"? What does it mean that they are "in Christ" (1:22)?

8. Is Paul's "assuring" the Galatians "before God" an oath
   (1:20)? If so, how is this compatible with Christ's words
   against oath taking (Matthew 5:33-37)?

Endnotes

1. George Croly, "Spirit of God, Descend upon My Heart," *Hymns of the Christian Life* (Camp Hill, PA: Christian Publications, 1978), # 137.
2. Robert Grant, "Almighty Lord, the Sun Shall Fail" (a hymn).

4

The Compatibility of Paul's Gospel

Galatians 2:1-10

Fourteen years later I went up again to Jerusalem, this time with Barnabas. I took Titus along also. I went in response to a revelation and set before them the gospel that I preach among the Gentiles. But I did this privately to those who seemed to be leaders, for fear that I was running or had run my race in vain. Yet not even Titus, who was with me, was compelled to be circumcised, even though he was a Greek. This matter arose because some false brothers had infiltrated our ranks to spy on the freedom we have in Christ Jesus and to make us slaves. We did not give in to them for a moment, so that the truth of the gospel might remain with you.

As for those who seemed to be important—whatever they were makes no difference to me; God does not judge by external appearance—those men added nothing to my message. On the contrary, they saw that I had been entrusted with the task of preaching the gospel to the Gentiles, just as Peter had been to the Jews. For God, who was at work in the ministry of Peter as an apostle to the Jews, was also at work in my ministry as an apostle to the Gentiles. James, Peter and John, those reputed to be pillars, gave me and Barnabas the right hand of fellowship when they recognized the

grace given to me. They agreed that we should go to the Gentiles,
and they to the Jews. All they asked was that we should continue to
remember the poor, the very thing I was eager to do.

Can God's people maintain true fellowship and at the same
time hold to differing emphases in ministry or lifestyle?
That is the question posed by this section. It is by no means a
problem Paul discovered. The tribes of Israel faced it as well
when they were conquering the land of Canaan (Numbers 32;
Joshua 22).

You will recall that on the eve of their crossing over the
River Jordan into Canaan several tribes asked Moses for per-
mission to settle in what has historically been called
Transjordan. Originally, there had been no provision for this in
the allotment of land by the Lord. Their request raised all sorts
of issues. Was it rebellion against the Lord and against the unity
of His people? Was it purely a selfish desire on the part of the
Transjordanian tribes? Was it an attempt to evade the rigors of
war and conquest?

Clearly, a settlement on the east bank of Jordan would involve a somewhat different style of living. Further, it would
separate those tribes from the main body of Israel by a natural
boundary, the Jordan River. It could even be taken as excluding
them from access to the main sanctuary of God to be established on the western side. And to make matters worse, the
Transjordanian tribes wanted to build their own altar to the
Lord. Would such an arrangement be workable? In short,
would the whole body of tribes be able to maintain true spiritual
fellowship with each other and yet acknowledge differences in
method and procedure?

Actually, the resolution of this issue sounds very much like
the way Paul discusses the resolution of the similar problem
facing himself and the Jerusalem Christian leaders. In the an-

cient situation, it was agreed that the settlement of the tribes could take place. The stipulations were that they would have to commit themselves to the faithful support of the conquest effort and they would have to guarantee that the Transjordanian altar would be only a *symbol* of the unity of the twelve tribes and not in any sense in competition to the main altar in Canaan.

Likewise, Paul and the other apostles will have to arrive at a common understanding of what is the proper basis of their fellowship in the gospel and what are the legitimate areas of differing emphasis. They too will make commitments to support the common cause.

Thus Paul turns at the opening of chapter 2 to an emphasis in the defense of his gospel that was somewhat different from the biographical approach he had taken in chapter 1. For although his gospel is correct, it is not by that fact necessarily incompatible with the gospel proclaimed by the key Christian leaders in Jerusalem.

Yet even though Paul's gospel is compatible with that of the Jerusalem apostles, it is transparently obvious to him and to the Galatians that it contains an emphasis that was not fully present in the gospel of the Jerusalem apostles. The emphasis on the right of Gentiles to accept Christ without becoming Jews was not in the preaching and teaching of church leaders like Peter, James and John—at least not to anywhere near the extent that such an emphasis was present in the thinking and teaching of Paul. Although Peter through his ministry to Cornelius may have been brought reluctantly to see that the gospel was for all nations and peoples (Acts 10:1 to 11:18), he did not seem to have developed that idea to the extent Paul had proclaimed it.

Paul's desire at this point is to show that, while he did not derive his gospel from the Jerusalem apostles, they fully endorsed his emphasis. But it is not as though he had to obtain their approval to validate his gospel. It is valid simply because it is God's gospel. However, Paul can certainly state for the benefit of the Galatians the fact that the other apostles had fully accepted his gospel. This would, he hoped, serve to enhance their estimate of the value of his ministry with them. If it was Jerusalem's perspective that Paul's gospel was fully compatible with the primitive Christian proclamation, why then shouldn't the Galatians treat it the same way?

Shoring up his argument, Paul recounts a key visit he made to Jerusalem in which this compatibility was made abundantly clear. Although the identification of the visit has been hotly debated by scholars, it may not be absolutely essential to identify the visit correctly if only we can appreciate that Paul's purpose in referring to it was to illustrate and prove the compatibility of the two gospels. Suffice it to say that the passage before us can profitably be understood as a reference to Paul's visit to Jerusalem to attend the Council reported in Acts 15.[1]

In any case, what we have in Galatians 2:1-10 is an attempt to demonstrate and elaborate this idea of the compatibility of Paul's gospel. We can detect three emphases: 1) his motive in going to Jerusalem was to demonstrate this compatibility, showing that compatibility between different proclaimers of the gospel is a desirable thing; 2) his manner in the discussion was one of unyielding firmness in opposing the forces destructive to God's gospel, attesting to the fact that compatibility between different proclaimers of the gospel does not at all mean that they would compromise its basic teachings; and 3) the result of his visit was a wonderful expression of the compatibility of Paul's gospel with that of the Christian authorities in Jerusalem, testifying that true compatibility will result in genuine fellowship.

Compatibility Should Be Sought: Paul's Motive (2:1-2)

On the surface, it would appear that Paul's visit to Jerusalem was motivated simply by the fact that God commanded him to go, since he says that the visit was in response to a divine revelation (2:2). However, the issue of Paul's motivation for the journey may not be quite as simple as that.

The fact that it was preceded by revelation does not necessarily eliminate the possibility that there were also other motives at work. In fact, it is not entirely clear that the revelation referred to consisted specifically of the command to go to Jerusalem. Alternatively, it may have been a renewed revelation of the importance of the ideas surrounding the Gentile mission and the inclusion of Gentile converts in the people of God apart from adherence to certain ceremonial aspects of the Mosaic law. The trip to Jerusalem might then be due to Paul's decision in response to these important truths.

Other considerations may also have been present in Paul's decision to make the visit. It seems evident from the whole passage that it was also Paul's intent to come to an agreement with the Christian leaders concerning his ministry. After more than a decade of relatively independent ministry, in which Paul's distinctive emphasis had been developed, the time was long overdue for an acknowledged understanding by all concerned respecting its status and legitimacy.

On the other hand, we should not understand his words "for fear that I was running or had run my race in vain" (2:2) to mean that he was ready to give up his distinctive ministry. Rather, they indicate that he wanted to be very open before those in Jerusalem and that he sensed the critical importance of the interchange. The nature of his ministry certainly was of the utmost concern to him. However, Paul had no doubt about the correctness of his position and of the persuasive arguments he could muster to support it.

Moreover, it is possible that Paul's taking the uncircumcised Gentile Christian Titus along with him (2:1) was designed to bring the issue to a clear focus. Would Titus, an already established and acknowledged Christian leader, be required to undergo circumcision to please a narrow Jewish-Christian perspective? This would be a perfect opportunity for that kind of question to be settled—hopefully once and for all.

However that may be, it seems beyond question that Paul intended this visit as a very crucial moment in establishing the compatibility of his gospel ministry and that of the Jerusalem branch of Christendom.

The desire for compatibility between Christian teachers stems, of course, from the more general ideal of the unity of all believers, for which the Lord Jesus prayed on the eve of His betrayal (John 17:20-23), and which Paul himself commanded (Ephesians 4:3).

Compatibility Does Not Mean Compromising the Gospel: Paul's Manner (Galatians 2:3-5)

But any compatibility that might be achieved and recognized would have to allow Paul to keep his understanding of the gospel for the Gentile world. Thus, Paul's argumentation in Jerusalem was firm, forcefully resisting the attempt to impose circumcision on Gentiles.

It is evident that the original opposition to Paul's outlook came not from the Jerusalem apostles themselves but from "false brothers." For Paul here says plainly, "This matter arose because some false brothers had infiltrated our ranks" (2:4).[2]

The term "false brothers" is an expression that is not without interpretive problems. From this particular combination of terms it is difficult, to say the least, to ascertain the precise way in which Paul viewed them. Were they Christians ("brothers") whose views were somewhat distorted? Or were they unbelievers ("false") posing as and erroneously claiming to be believers in Christ?

The latter interpretation of their status appears to be supported by Paul's use of the terms "infiltrated," "spy" and "make us slaves," which seem to be more appropriate in reference to those who ultimately are to be considered to be unbelievers, despite their profession to the contrary. Perhaps it does not really matter. Nor can we say, at least not from this text, what their motives might have been. What is clear is that Paul forcefully and unflinchingly withstood them and their theology.

What is more, it is extremely unlikely that Paul was silent and passive in the discussion that must have ensued and that led to the decision not to require Titus to be circumcised.[3] The text records nothing of the discussion that must have taken place, but Paul almost certainly spoke out on such an issue, especially if he had intentionally brought Titus along for the possibility—even the probability—of just such a confrontation. The fact that no details regarding the discussion are given certainly does not mean that there was no discussion; the interchange was most likely rather heated.

We learn also that for Paul everything was at stake in this encounter. The very truth of the gospel was at stake, the very freedom that we have in Christ. This was no casual incident in Paul's career, included simply to be exhaustive in the recounting of his contacts with Jerusalem so his opponents might not be able to accuse him of leaving out some "crucial" detail. Rather, it was a momentous event in which all that had been revealed to Paul and all that he was committed to in ministry were up for debate.

No wonder, then, that his manner was firm in opposition to these false brothers. He was uncompromising when it came to something that touched the heart of the gospel as he understood it. True, as we will shortly see, he could be quite charitable and open to cooperation where subordinate issues were in question. But when it involved matters central to the gospel faith, there was absolutely no room for compromise.

In this regard, Paul was like the Old Testament prophets, who were fearless in their stand for the word of God. One thinks, for example, of Micaiah, perhaps reticent at first, or at least superficially so, to speak with boldness to King Ahab, but then not reluctant in the least to stand for the right in denouncing the king's prophets and predicting disaster for the nation (1 Kings 22).

At first King Ahab was hesitant to ask Micaiah for guidance because Micaiah had a reputation for predicting calamity. But when the king finally asked Micaiah whether Israel should go into battle against Ramoth Gilead, the answer he received from the prophet was a favorable one: "Attack and be victorious, . . . for the LORD will give it into the king's hand" (22:15). Suspicious of such an answer from this man of God, the king pressed him further, and then the prophet's dismal but truthful message was given: "I saw all Israel scattered on the hills like sheep without a shepherd" (22:17). Ultimately, Micaiah, as God's prophet, had to proclaim His message uncompromisingly, even though it was not a positive one.

Yes, there are times when there can be no compromise, and Paul had a sense that this was one of those moments. We too need a spirit of discernment to know what is an appropriate occasion to stand uncompromisingly for principle and when to conclude that the issues in question are peripheral.

Compatibility Results in Genuine Fellowship (Galatians 2:6-10)

The result was exactly what Paul had hoped for and intended—the recognition by the apostles of the compatibility of his gospel with that of the Jerusalem church leadership. This recognition of the compatibility of the two "gospels," if we may call them such—they were really not two gospels but two ministries of the same gospel—was expressed by a union of hands: the right hand(s) of fellowship. But beneath that symbolism lay the acknowledgment that indeed God's grace was at work in the ministry of Paul and even that he was His apostle, as they were.

Furthermore, demonstration of the solidarity between the two branches of ministry (to Jew and to Gentile) was to be continued in the future by Paul's commitment to remember—that is, materially support—the poorer Jewish Christians in Jerusalem and Judea, who had by this time suffered persecution at the hands of Jews who were hostile to the Christian message. There is a note of poignancy here, in that Paul himself had earlier been partially responsible for the oppression of Jewish Christians throughout the area that undoubtedly contributed to their present state of material need. Perhaps this played a role in Paul's substantial interest in bringing aid to these struggling Judean saints.

It is also worth noting just how important in Paul's thinking was the issue of material support of the Jerusalem church. This present concern to assist the impoverished community of Judean believers had been preceded by an effort to relieve their situation in a time of famine (Acts 11:28-30), and subsequently his burden for contributing to the needs of the poor became an all-consuming passion. This concern resulted in his collecting funds from the Gentile churches to help their Palestinian brothers in Christ (Acts 24:17; 1 Corinthians 16:1; 2 Corinthians 8–9). Indeed, this is fellowship—sharing—at a most practical level.

We may also note in passing the renewed claim that Paul's gospel owed nothing substantive to the teaching or authority of the Jerusalem apostles. Paul was undoubtedly in touch with "apostolic teaching." The pattern of the apostles' proclamation, the *kerygma,* is abundantly evident in the record given by Luke in the book of Acts (10:36-43). Thus the period of Old Testament preparation, the Spirit-empowered, miracle-working ministry of Christ, the suffering, death and burial, and particularly the resurrection—all of these were elements common to both the preaching of the Jerusalem-centered apostles and that of Paul.

But as connected to these themes as Paul clearly was, his gospel, his unique emphases, even some of the distinctive terminology were his, derived from God and born out of the individual circumstances of his life and ministry.

Compatibility does not imply any cookie-cutter sameness that does not tolerate individual differences. The New Testament offers abundant examples of cordiality and cooperation that still leave room for differences within limits.

Paul's discussion in First Corinthians 3, for example, reveals his sense of compatibility between Apollos and himself, while at the same time granting certain differences in ministry. "The Lord has assigned to each his task. I planted the seed, Apollos watered it, but God made it grow" (3:5-6).

Likewise, it is the clear implication in his discussions concerning spiritual gifts that there are individual differences and that these differences exist under the sovereignty of the divine Spirit. Yet it is equally clear that the differences should work together in cooperation and harmony rather than in competition (12:4-26).

These examples, of course, are about areas of ministry. But the same idea holds true in areas that are much more theologically oriented, as long as the issue is not central or essential to the Christian faith. Thus there is a toleration as to what a person may hold regarding details of diet and the observance of festival days. Even though technically a more enlightened position on these matters may be ultimately correct, still a stricter interpretation of the requirements is permissible for those who cannot see the issue in a more knowledgeable and therefore less inhibiting manner. There is certainly room here for deviation in nonessentials (Romans 14:1-8). The two perspectives are compatible in the sense that individuals holding the positions may and should otherwise be in complete harmony with each other, respecting the right of others to live in accordance with the dictates of their conscience before God.

Conclusion

Earlier, we noted the prophet Micaiah as an example of a man of God who would not ultimately compromise his God-given message. Better yet is the example of Jeremiah, who entirely dispensed with any pretense of courtly courtesy and boldly proclaimed the destruction of the Lord's temple, completely contradicting the false prophets who proclaimed peace when there was no peace (Jeremiah 7:1-11). So bold was his preaching that he nearly lost his life in the course of standing for the truth.

We should never minimize the need for compatibility and unity in the body of Christ. Moreover, our commitment to the unity of the church should ever take tangible forms of expression in ministering to the material needs of those fellow believers who are less fortunate than we. But on the other hand, we, like Paul, should never sacrifice the doctrinal purity of our common faith on the altar of expediency or an artificial unity. There may be occasions on which doctrine will take precedence over formal collegiality.

Perhaps a recent development in the world of academia will suffice to illustrate what this desired harmony of differing perspectives might mean. Evangelical theologians are divided into many camps when it comes to matters of the Bible's teachings concerning prophecy, the future coming of Christ and the nature of the kingdom of God. Two of these schools of thought are known respectively as the Dispensational interpretation of Scripture and Covenant theology. There was a time when the differences were so sharp and the feelings so strong that the two groups had more or less to agree to disagree in order to get along with each other at professional conferences.

But somewhat recently key representatives of the two per-spectives have been making a sincere attempt to see things from the other point of view. First a few Dispensational schol-ars began to make changes in regard to their understanding of the kingdom of God, so that this understanding came to look more and more like that of the Covenant theologians. Then a leading spokesman for the Covenant theology position re-sponded by espousing an understanding of the kingdom that sounded a good bit more like Dispensationalism than Covenant theologians had been accustomed to doing.

The result has been a renewed respect for the opponents' posi-tion and the beginnings of a fruitful dialogue between the two camps. There is still not a complete unanimity, but there is a de-cided reconciliation. And it does not really matter for our purposes here which side in the debate has the better understanding theolog-ically. What matters is that the two camps have sought and achieved a greater measure of compatibility. Moreover, it is strik-ing that the questions that are in dispute do not touch the heart of the gospel, just as the differences between Paul and the Jerusalem apostles were not over the central issues of Christian doctrine. Just as different perspectives were recognized as compatible in the first century—as long as essential doctrines were not compromised—so ought it to be in the third millennium.

Isn't this what Paul calls us to when he commands believers to speak the truth in love (Ephesians 4:15)? We ought never to compromise the truth, and so we are committed to speaking it. But truth must be spoken in love, a love that fosters unity be-tween believers, whatever differences they may have in details. Maintaining the balance between truth and love constitutes the true maturity of the deeper Christian life.

How good a thing it is, how pleasant to behold—
    when brethren learn to live as one, the law of love
        uphold.

As perfume, by its scent, breathes fragrance all
    around,
so life itself will sweeter be where unity is found.
And like refreshing dew that falls upon the hills,
    true union sheds its gentle grace and deeper love
    instills.
God grants His choicest gifts to those who live in
    peace.
To them His blessings shall abound and evermore
    increase.[4]

Questions for Reflection or Discussion

1. What was the content of the revelation to Paul (Galatians 2:2)?
2. How strong should we understand the sense of the word "fear" (2:2)?
3. How should the wording about Titus not being compelled to be circumcised be understood (2:3)?
4. How should the issue involved in the phrase "false brothers" be resolved (2:4)?
5. What did Paul mean by calling Peter an apostle to the Jews and himself an apostle to the Gentiles (2:8)?
6. What is implied in calling James, Peter and John "those reputed to be pillars" (2:9)? Is Paul disparaging them?

Endnotes

1. For a full discussion of the problems and the position here taken, see Moises Silva, *Explorations in Exegetical Method: Galatians as a Test Case* (Grand Rapids: Baker Books, 1996), 132-138.
2. A similar, but clearly not identical, situation is envisioned in Acts 15:1. Note that in that passage the false teaching takes place in Antioch rather

than in Galatia, and the teachers are more specifically identified as men from Judea.

3. There is some ambiguity in the wording. Are we to understand that Titus did not here undergo circumcision? Or did Paul mean to imply that Titus did receive circumcision but did so willingly and not by being compelled to? The former seems preferable.

4. James E. Seddon, "How Good a Thing It Is, How Pleasant to Behold" (a hymn).

5

The Consistency
of Paul's Gospel

Galatians 2:11-21

When Peter came to Antioch, I opposed him to his face, because he was clearly in the wrong. Before certain men came from James, he used to eat with the Gentiles. But when they arrived, he began to draw back and separate himself from the Gentiles because he was afraid of those who belonged to the circumcision group. The other Jews joined him in his hypocrisy, so that by their hypocrisy even Barnabas was led astray.

When I saw that they were not acting in line with the truth of the gospel, I said to Peter in front of them all, "You are a Jew, yet you live like a Gentile and not like a Jew. How is it, then, that you force Gentiles to follow Jewish customs?

"We who are Jews by birth and not 'Gentile sinners' know that a man is not justified by observing the law, but by faith in Jesus Christ. So we, too, have put our faith in Christ Jesus that we may be justified by faith in Christ and not by observing the law, because by observing the law no one will be justified.

"If, while we seek to be justified in Christ, it becomes evident that we ourselves are sinners, does that mean that Christ promotes sin? Absolutely not! If I rebuild what I destroyed, I prove that I am

a lawbreaker. For through the law I died to the law so that I might live for God. I have been crucified with Christ and I no longer live, but Christ lives in me. The life I live in the body, I live by faith in the Son of God, who loved me and gave himself for me. I do not set aside the grace of God, for if righteousness could be gained through the law, Christ died for nothing!"

Is the way we treat people consistent with the faith we profess? That is one of the key issues posed by this section. And there is no better example of one whose treatment of others was consistent with faith than the life of one of the greatest but most undercelebrated figures in the Old Testament.

Ruth was originally not one of the people of God, but rather a Moabitess by birth and culture. What drew her to embrace the God of Israel is necessarily a matter of speculation: it may have been the attractiveness of the spiritual life and character of the Israelite family into which she had married. But whatever the motives and antecedents, her conversion to Israel's God was surely genuine. It is forever enshrined in her classic words, "Thy people shall be my people, and thy God my God" (Ruth 1:16, KJV). There was absolutely nothing inferior about this profession of faith.

Did it issue in works of charity toward others? We do not need to be reminded of her selfless devotion to her unfortunate mother-in-law, Naomi. Ruth was not compelled by any external factor to leave her homeland for a life of hard work to support Naomi. She could have stayed back in familiar and comfortable surroundings in Moab, as did her sister-in-law Orpah. But no, she was committed through and through to helping the helpless, committed to long days of grueling, back-breaking work in the hot sun, gleaning sheaves of grain for the most meager of results, all to fulfill what she took to be a labor of love for Naomi.

That is the kind of consistency between faith and works of love that the author of Galatians was concerned about. And so Paul uses another important event from his life as a negative example of consistency, an incident in which he criticizes Peter's hypocrisy.

In this account Paul shows the Galatians that Peter actually held the same faith in Christ as Paul did and (in theory at least) the same theological position as Paul—namely, that Gentiles could become followers of Christ without being required to conform to Jewish laws and practices. It was not in faith or theology that they differed. Rather, it was Peter's failure to practice that faith and theology consistently. Paul saw this inconsistency clearly and uses it now in his argument to point out to the Galatians how they should *not* act.

Let us consider, then, the need for consistency between our practice and our faith, the maintenance of this consistency through the confrontation and correction of inconsistency, and finally the foundational truths of the gospel that emphasize the importance of such consistency.

Necessity of Consistency (Galatians 2:11-13)

The main point was that however orthodox Peter was in his theology, his practice was not always consistent with that theology. More specifically, it was not his practice in general that was open to challenge. Rather, it was his *shift* in practice that was questionable—the shift to a particularly hypocritical practice which was inconsistent with his previous pattern of behavior. Previously he had eaten with the Gentile believers, but then he ceased this practice when the delegation from Jerusalem arrived on the scene (2:12). This group held a much stricter interpretation of the place of Gentile Christians.

Moreover, the fact that (according to Paul) Peter had acted out of fear of this delegation made Peter's shift in practice the more reprehensible (2:12-13). It would be bad enough just to engage in behavior inconsistent with one's beliefs. But to do so from fear of people who are themselves in the wrong seems to be doubly reproachable.

Fear is a strong motivational force. It can motivate one toward improvement or at least the maintenance of qualities that are considered good and beneficial. After all, "the fear of the LORD is the beginning of wisdom" (Psalm 111:10). But fear can also provide the impulse to depart from the good, and that is what happened to Peter on this occasion.

Peter, of course, does not stand alone in yielding to the impulse of fear. All of the disciples joined him in forsaking their master at the moment of His arrest (Mark 14:50), and even after His crucifixion they were gathered in an upper room out of fear of the Jewish authorities (John 20:19). Additionally, at least one of Jesus' followers, Joseph of Arimathea, allowed fear to keep him from standing up for his Lord for quite some time, as he is described as a disciple of Jesus, albeit secretly for fear of the authorities (19:38). More parallel to Peter's action, in the harm that it brought to another, is that of the parents of the man born blind, who out of fear placed the onus of responding to the authorities on their son (9:20-23).

It must be admitted that the inconsistency detected by Paul was rather subtle. In fact, it was so subtle that it confused even Paul's companion in ministry, Barnabas. Nevertheless, to Paul it was inconsistent for Peter initially to treat the Gentile Christians as Christians on the same footing as Jewish Christians by eating with them, thus disregarding Jewish scruples about eating with Gentiles, and then reverse this practice, thus relegating them to inferior status. Paul calls Peter's behavior hypocritical (Galatians 2:13).

What made matters worse was Peter's position of influence, whereby others ("other Jews") were led into the same inconsistency (2:13). Naturally, one does not have to be in a position of authority to have undesirable influence on others. For instance, Paul's remarks about how we should be concerned for the spiritual fragility of the weaker brother (Romans 14; 1 Corinthians 8–10) apply to all the people of God.

But what is true in general for us all is especially applicable to someone in a role of leadership. That is why the king was so important in ancient Israelite society. What the king did was a model, either positively or negatively, that his subjects naturally followed. Jeroboam, for example, in condoning idolatrous worship in Bethel and Dan, was the cause of all Israel sinning against the Lord (1 Kings 12:26-33).

Consistency between the content of the gospel and our behavior is essential, says Paul. In fact, is it any stretch of the truth to suggest that consistency between faith and practice is one of the hallmarks of the deeper life? Surely one cannot legitimately claim to be experiencing deeper life in Christ without such consistency between one's beliefs and their outworking in practical ways.

Maintenance of Consistency (Galatians 2:14)

But consistency between practice and faith is not something that can be achieved once and for all. It is something that must be preserved and maintained, and when it is not maintained, there may need to be recourse to a gentle confrontation. While Paul was not necessarily absolutely consistent in his every action, we do see that here in this particular instance Paul's application of the gospel was consistent with his theology. From this high moral ground Paul could point out Peter's inconsistency and, by implication, his own consistency in applying the gospel of salvation by faith.

Paul's challenge to Peter not only called into question Peter's own inconsistency between freely fellowshiping with Gentile believers ("live like a Gentile") and then withdrawing from that practice. Peter's separation had also forced the Gentile brothers to separate from Jewish believers, that is, to follow Jewish-style separation practices.

We see again how far-reaching for others are the implications of our actions. In the case of Barnabas following Peter in his hypocritical action, he at least could have resisted Peter's example if he had chosen to do so. But the Gentile Christians at Antioch really had no option but to suffer the rejection and second-class status brought about by Peter's hypocrisy.

What a shame when our actions bring about for others the pain of social rejection, especially when the injured party is completely innocent of any wrongdoing whatsoever, as it was in this case. The only thing that at all mitigates Peter's injury to the Gentiles is that the result of Paul's rebuke may well have been another reversal on Peter's part, restoring the marred fellowship with the Gentile believers.

A similar situation, in which an innocent person suffers because of some other party's hypocritical act of rejection, may be found in Jane Austen's *Pride and Prejudice*. Specifically, it involves Charles Bingley's hurtful actions toward Jane Bennet, the oldest of the five unmarried daughters in the Bennet family.

Mr. and Mrs. Bennet are a most unlikely couple, he being scholarly and logical in his approach to any of life's problems and she flighty, emotional and scheming, almost totally consumed with the successful marrying off of her five daughters. They have no real common ground. And yet it was in just this at least mildly dysfunctional household that daughter Jane developed into a remarkably delightful person—pleasant, considerate, generous—in a word, guileless.

Young bachelor gentleman Charles Bingley's arrival to take up residence as the Bennets' new neighbor provided Mrs. Bennet with her golden opportunity to play matchmaker for Jane. In fact, the match was a good one, as Charles and Jane were drawn together and progressively found delight in each other's company. They would make a handsome couple—until Bingley, though inwardly still fond of her but swayed by his friend Fitzwilliam Darcy's influence, abruptly cut off his friendship with Jane and left his country residence to take up life in London.

Needless to say, Jane was perplexed and devastated. Without any explanation for Bingley's actions, she felt completely rejected, cut off from the fellowship she had so recently enjoyed. She suffered indeed through Bingley's callous neglect. Of course, much later, Bingley recognized the error of his cruel and hypocritical action and the couple was restored in fellowship and eventually in marriage. But in the meantime, his vacillation, like Peter's, had brought needless suffering to an innocent party.

As for the style of Paul's confrontation of Peter, it was both direct ("to his face" Galatians 2:11) and public ("in front of them all," 2:14). But confrontation may not always need to take this bold a form. A softer, more mellow approach is also possible. In this regard Paul's dealing with Philemon is revealing.

The issue was how to get Philemon, a well-to-do Christian, to receive Onesimus back as a brother in Christ. Onesimus was not only Philemon's slave, but he had run away from his master. There was no reason for Philemon to forgive the past—except that Onesimus had become a follower of Christ—and even then, Philemon's willingness to receive his former slave would not necessarily be without any problem.

Paul, of course, could have confronted Philemon forcefully and commanded him to accede to his wishes. Instead, his confrontation took the form of an appeal (Philemon 8-10): "Therefore, although in Christ I could be bold and order you to do what you ought to do, yet I appeal to you on the basis of love. I then, as Paul—an old man and now also a prisoner of Christ Jesus—I appeal to you for my son Onesimus."

In a very practical way Paul accompanies his appeal with a promise to underwrite any expenses that Philemon has incurred as a result of his being inconvenienced and injured by Onesimus' actions. It may be that Paul thought Philemon would forego his offer, but in any case, he apparently makes the offer in good faith (Philemon 18).

Foundation of Consistency (Galatians 2:15-21)

It is in the second half of our passage that we find Paul's discussion of the gospel—the gospel that both he and Peter, as well as the rest of the early apostles and their faithful followers, held in common. This gospel itself provides the foundational truths that emphasize the need for consistency.

It is clear from this account that Peter held essentially the same beliefs as Paul regarding the requirements for salvation, even the salvation of Gentiles. Paul assumes Peter's agreement when he talks about their common belief in justification by faith in 2:15-16. In that passage Paul expresses the conviction that the doctrine of justification by faith, apart from works of the law, was a common possession and understanding of both Gentile and Jewish Christianity. As far as their beliefs are concerned, there was no disagreement between Paul and Peter.

Paul goes on to draw out the depths of this concept in the succeeding verses (2:17-21). While some of the logic in these and subsequent words may be a little obscure, there is no doubt that the general sense is a commitment to the principle of salvation through faith rather than the works of the law.

However, while the principle of salvation by faith is simple and clear, it must not be oversimplified. There is ever the risk of oversimplifying and watering down the biblical concept of faith. Biblical saving faith, while simple, is not thereby nebulous, but has a number of important implications that Paul alludes to here.

First, salvation by faith implies that we must own up to our sinfulness. In fact, in the context of having just mentioned "Gentile sinners" (2:15) this admission amounts to accepting the fact that all people, Jew or Gentile, are on the same level before God. Jews are no less sinful than Gentiles are. Both Jew and Gentile stand in the same need of salvation, and they all must receive that salvation only through faith in Christ.

Secondly, one implication that ought *not* to be drawn from the idea that we are in need of salvation by faith is that such a doctrine somehow involves God or Christ as the cause of our sin or the approver of our sin. Paul, of course, finds such a notion preposterous and absolutely abhorrent. God forbid it (2:17)! We are lawbreakers because it is we who break the law of God (2:18).

Third, Paul guards very carefully against having the concept of faith interpreted in too casual a manner (2:19-20). Rather, he insists that to accept Christ by faith is an extremely radical act. It is to be crucified with Christ and thus to die to the law or, for that matter, to any other theoretically conceivable means of approach to God. In one sense faith is more radical and difficult than keeping the law. As difficult as keeping the law is—for truly to keep it one must keep it in its entirety—it requires only obedience, after all.

Faith, on the other hand, requires crucifixion with Christ, or death to self. Naturally, Paul does not mean this in any literal sense, as he goes on to talk about living in the body. Nevertheless, faith requires a radical death with Christ, and that is a difficult move for any human to accept. There is particularly a resistance to it in the mind of modern man, who does not want to admit weakness, moral frailty or any need for depending on the help of a higher being. In fact, such a radical move as self-crucifixion cannot be accepted, says Paul, apart from the grace of God that enables it (2:21).

But the issue of crucifixion with Christ is not something that can be bypassed; it is part and parcel of Paul's view of salvation and life in Christ. He not only touches on it here but also develops it more extensively in Romans 6: We died with Christ, were baptized into His death, and were united with Him in His death (Romans 6:3-14). Moreover, it is likely that our crucifixion with the Savior is what Paul has in mind when he talks about our being circumcised with the circumcision of Christ (Colossians 2:11-12). So the whole idea of the believer's death with the Lord Jesus is quite fundamental in Paul's outlook: "I am crucified with Christ" (Galatians 2:20, KJV).

It is widely recognized that in this concept of being crucified with Christ we have what may be called the essence of the deeper life. What may not be so commonly acknowledged is that this crucifixion with Christ and the death to self that it implies are integrally bound up with the conversion experience (Romans 6:3-4). This is not to deny that there are moments after one's conversion when spiritual self-crucifixion is a meaningful mode of experience. It is to say, however, that in one sense the deeper life is so tied to the initial moment of the Christian life—conversion—that it may rightly be thought of as a deeper appreciation for the spiritual realities that are inherent, potentially at least, in the very beginnings of Christian experience.

Conclusion

We began this chapter with the story of Ruth, as an example of works of love that are truly consistent with the profession of faith. Along the same line, we cannot fail to mention the story of the Good Samaritan, who again poured out his life, including his possessions, on behalf of a needy soul (Luke 10:30-35). We know the account well, and we note simply the following high points.

The Samaritan's concern for the robbery victim was born out of love and pity, which he expressed with a great deal of personal care by medicating and treating the man's wounds. His kindness cost him time, as it presumably slowed up his journey. Likewise, it cost him money. And it was a sustained interest, as he was committed to following up on the victim's progress. Truly, the story's hero was putting into practice the theology embraced by the second great commandment: "You shall love your neighbor."

What is most remarkable about both of these individuals is that they are examples of Gentiles expressing their faith consistently toward Jews, whereas Peter the Jew had difficulty in expressing his faith consistently toward his Gentile brothers. Peter's shame is, therefore, all the greater.

On the other hand, many characters in the Bible fail to measure up to expected standards but really cannot be called inconsistent since they had no true faith to begin with. We think, for example, of Judas or Demas or perhaps Saul in the Old Testament.[1]

But an interesting example of the type represented by Peter in this section is the figure of John Mark. There can be no serious question about his genuine commitment to the gospel teaching. From a Christian home (Acts 12:12), commended by both Paul (2 Timothy 4:11) and Peter (1 Peter 5:13), author of the second Gospel—surely nobody wants to claim him as another Judas or Demas. And yet his devotion to the gospel ministry at one point wavered (Acts 15:38), and once again Paul engaged in the role of confronter, refusing to take him as coworker in his second missionary journey. On that occasion the issue was not nearly as central to sound theology as at the present circumstance. Yet Paul stood up to Barnabas rather strongly over John Mark's unsuitability as a traveling companion and team member.[2]

In fact, Peter himself, on another occasion, displayed the same kind of weakness in failing to bring profession and practice together consistently. Surely Peter was at heart a true follower of Christ, but his denials of Christ (Matthew 26:69-75) were completely inconsistent with his supposed commitment to the Savior. Yet once again the situation met with perfect resolution, as Peter's guilt and shame were ministered to by the master Confronter, and Peter repented and was restored (John 21:15-19).

A final issue is how we should respond when a brother fails in his obligation to act consistently. Sometimes it is necessary to admonish or rebuke a fellow believer. It is worth noting, however, that such a confrontational approach to correcting a brother must be done humbly and cautiously as well as in the conviction that we clearly have the mind of the Lord. In fact, it would be wise to consider whether a more indirect approach to "confrontation" would be advisable, along the lines of Paul's dealings with Philemon. In this regard, the proverb is no doubt appropriate: "A gentle answer turns away wrath" (Proverbs 15:1).

Meanwhile, we ourselves are obligated, whether we confront or not, to maintain a reasonable consistency between our faith and our practice, for our own spiritual well-being, for the sake of others who may be influenced by our actions, and ultimately for the glory of the God of Jew and Gentile alike. Such consistency will be a mark of maturity in Christ, a true sign that we are experiencing the deeper life as it was meant to be lived.

> Plead we now for faith alone,
>   faith which by our works is shown,
> Active faith, that makes us whole,
>   forms the Savior in the soul.
> Let us for this faith contend.
>   Sure salvation is its end.

Let us never from it move,
saved by faith which works by love.[3]

Questions for Reflection or Discussion

1. What was the nature of Paul's opposing Peter to his face (Galatians 2:11)? Was it private or simply direct?
2. What is implied in the expression "*used to* eat" (2:12)?
3. Who were the "other Jews" who imitated Peter (2:13)?
4. What does it mean to say that "Barnabas was led astray" (2:13)?
5. How does Paul's confronting Peter "in front of them all" (2:14) agree with Jesus' instructions in Matthew 18:15-17?
6. Is there significance in Paul's shifting from "we" (2:17) to "I" (2:18)? If so, what is it?
7. In what sense does one die to the law (2:19)?
8. What is the significance of "have been" in "I have been crucified" (2:20)?
9. How should the debate between "faith in" (NIV) and "faith of" (KJV) be resolved (2:20)?
10. In 2:21 Paul says, "if righteousness could be gained through the law . . ." Is he assuming it could or could not be gained this way? Why?
11. How much of 2:14-21 are Paul's words to Peter? (See NIV quotation marks and footnote.)

Endnotes

1. Saul's spiritual condition is open to debate. But it is perhaps significant that his name is omitted from the list of the faithful in Hebrews 11.
2. In Acts 13:13, Luke's statement is rather bland, but in 15:38 he, no doubt reflecting Paul's perspective, charges John Mark with desertion.
3. Charles Wesley, "Let Us Join—'Tis God Commands" (a hymn).

6

The Heart of Paul's Gospel

Galatians 3:1-14

You foolish Galatians! Who has bewitched you? Before your very eyes Jesus Christ was clearly portrayed as crucified. I would like to learn just one thing from you: Did you receive the Spirit by observing the law, or by believing what you heard? Are you so foolish? After beginning with the Spirit, are you now trying to attain your goal by human effort? Have you suffered so much for nothing—if it really was for nothing? Does God give you his Spirit and work miracles among you because you observe the law, or because you believe what you heard?

Consider Abraham: "He believed God, and it was credited to him as righteousness." Understand, then, that those who believe are children of Abraham. The Scripture foresaw that God would justify the Gentiles by faith, and announced the gospel in advance to Abraham: "All nations will be blessed through you." So those who have faith are blessed along with Abraham, the man of faith.

All who rely on observing the law are under a curse, for it is written: "Cursed is everyone who does not continue to do everything written in the Book of the Law." Clearly no one is justified before God by the law, because, "The righteous will live by faith." The law is not based on faith; on the contrary, "The man who does these things will live by them." Christ redeemed us from the curse of the law by becoming a curse for us, for it is written: "Cursed is

everyone who is hung on a tree." He redeemed us in order that the
blessing given to Abraham might come to the Gentiles through
Christ Jesus, so that by faith we might receive the promise of the
Spirit.

"Justification by faith" may be a phrase that rolls easily off the tongue, but what does it really mean? More pointedly, why is it that some people cannot accept such an idea? The answer to this question is that the concept is almost totally opposed to the universally human tendency to want to feel autonomous, to believe that nothing comes from nothing, so that any spiritual benefit we may posses must naturally have been earned. But this is not the way of the gospel. Countless individuals throughout history have given testimony to the acceptance of this gospel teaching of justification by faith in Christ.

In fact, Martin Luther himself, the man for whom this doctrine became so meaningful that he started the Protestant Reformation, is a perfect example of just what the teaching can do in a human life and how transforming its influence can be. For some years Luther had followed the teachings of Christianity and the church, even to the point of becoming a priest, a monk and a teacher of theology. He faithfully practiced the teachings of the Christian faith as he understood them and was taught them, and he engaged in disciplined penitential activities for the forgiveness of his sins and the comfort of his soul; yet he still had not come to enjoy peace with God—until, that is, the magnificent truth of simply trusting in Christ for salvation broke in upon his understanding and he became a changed man, a new creature in Christ, forgiven of sin, justified by faith alone.

Up to this point in the epistle Paul has been defending his gospel by demonstrating that it is of God and that the Jerusalem apostles affirm rather than deny its validity. Now he turns to the heart of the issue—a defense of the doctrine of justification by faith.

This doctrine is continuously put forward in contrast to the competing philosophy of religion that maintains that keeping the law is necessary for salvation. Theoretically at least, there are then two ways: the way of faith and the way of works. But of course there is no doubt where Paul stands on the issue. Time after time he supports the way of faith and rejects the way of works.

In the development of this central theme there is considerable repetition of points. Paul weaves key terms together again and again in an overlapping argument. Nevertheless, a few stages in the argument can be identified. In this section he defends the doctrine of justification by faith first by means of reference to the Galatians' experience and then by the evidence of Scripture.

Before we trace these arguments, however, let us examine briefly some of the key terms used in Paul's discussion. Among others, these include the terms "righteousness," "blessing," "curse," "Spirit" and "faith."

Fundamental to Paul's attitude is the idea that sinful humanity stands in need of a position of righteousness or justification before God (3:11). This is the righteousness that God credited to Abraham's account through Abraham's faith (3:6), and that He planned for the Gentiles to receive as a gift from God (3:8).

This position of righteousness before God is His chief blessing to Abraham and his spiritual descendants. The blessing was indeed given to Abraham (3:14) but was clearly intended also to be enjoyed by the nations of the earth (3:8-9).

Since the opposite of blessing is a curse, those who are blessed with God's righteousness are also redeemed from the curse of the law (3:13). And since the curse involves death, the blessing is one that results in life (3:11).

Further, all of this blessing of righteousness is made possible on God's side by the work of His Spirit, whose influence is made prominent by continual mention at many points in the section (3:2, 3, 5, 14). The connection between the Spirit and righteousness is made clear by the parallelism of the clauses in 3:14. There "that the blessing given to Abraham might come to the Gentiles through Christ Jesus" is parallel to "so that by faith we might receive the promise of the Spirit." That is, the blessing given to Abraham, which is righteousness, is closely connected with receiving the Spirit.

On the human side, the work of God is received, as we have said, through faith. This too is a constant emphasis in the section. Sometimes it is just faith itself that is mentioned (3:6-8, 11, 12, 14). But at other points Paul is careful to indicate what is the proper object of this faith: naturally, the gospel—"what you heard" (3:2, 5).

Way of Faith

By this time it is no secret that Paul will urge upon his readers this cardinal doctrine of justification by faith. To defend the doctrine, he develops his discussion along three lines. First, he appeals to the Galatians' own experience, then to the experience of Abraham, and finally to that of the prophet Habakkuk.

Experience of the Galatians (3:1-5)

Paul begins his argument at the personal level. The apostle's passionate concern for the Galatians is obvious in his language that is intended to shock them to their senses, calling them foolish, bewitched (3:1), even seeming for a moment to suggest that their experience of the gospel was not real but amounting to nothing (3:4).

The first two of these expressions are intriguing, the first ("foolish") seeming to point to the Galatians' own responsibility and involvement in departing from the gospel they had received. To reject Christ and His gospel salvation is nothing if it is not the height of willful foolishness.

The second one, however, appears to suggest that there were other forces at work and that the Galatians had been duped, or "bewitched" and led astray.

Both perspectives are of course correct. The Galatians have indeed chosen to set aside the claims of Christ, but they did so under the influence of suggestion and perhaps even social pressure. In this way, the present description of their situation is roughly parallel to the situation in the primeval Garden. There too the departure from God had both internal (the free choice by Adam and Eve) and external (the suggestion by the Serpent) causes (Genesis 3).

That the third description of the Galatians is not intended by Paul to be taken completely literally is shown in his immediate qualification "if it really was for nothing." He gives them the benefit of the doubt and, for the moment at least, assumes the validity of their conversion experience.

Paul, however, can add logic to his passion. He does this first by drawing a contrast between the beginning of their Christian experience and the way they are trying to continue that experience and bring it to completion.[1] At every point, Paul maintains, their experience was based on faith, not on the keeping of the law through human effort (Galatians 3:2-3).

How did they receive the gospel? Was it not by faith? Of course it was. It was by a simple act of accepting the message, uncluttered by the necessity to do anything but repent of their unbelief and embrace the saving truth. The gospel they received had been imparted to them by an eminently clear presentation of the true gospel of Jesus Christ crucified for their sins (3:1), and the simplicity of the message demanded a corresponding simplicity of response in faith.

But while the act of believing in the good news was in one way simple, it did cost them dearly ("you suffered," 3:4) in terms of rejection and ridicule from their neighbors.[2] But they had apparently been willing at that time to bear that cost. How could they now think of casting such hard-won experience aside?

Further, God was obviously at work among the Galatians in mighty ways ("miracles," 3:5). Were they now going to turn their backs on all this experience as if it had never existed? Who in their right mind would cast off the blessings of the gospel? In fact, Paul's point is that the Galatians do not seem to be any longer in their right minds. They have been led astray by false teaching that was apparently made to appear very logical and even scripturally based.

The other extremely important and essential thought Paul develops in this section concerns the role of God's Holy Spirit. He talks of their receiving the Spirit (3:2), of their beginning with the Spirit (3:3) and of their being given the Spirit (3:5). In the light of other Pauline passages, such as Romans 8:9, this surely refers to the fact that the believer has the Spirit as an indwelling presence from the moment of conversion. However much the life of the Spirit needs to be cultivated and developed, the believer is from the beginning a person of the Spirit and therefore in a real sense a spiritual person.

Once again we can appreciate the fact that the deeper life is intimately connected with the inception of the Christian life. However greatly our Christian experience may be opened up to new vistas of understanding of God's purposes for us and to fresh responses to that understanding, faith undergirds it all. It may be that in our attempt to be precise in our description of the stages and developments of the Christian life we run the risk of blinding ourselves to its underlying simplicity. It is a life of faith—from the beginning to the end.

Experience of Abraham (Galatians 3:6-9)

The principle of faith is next illustrated in reference to Abraham, a model to be imitated by all true people of God: "Those who believe are children of Abraham" (3:7). Paul quotes from the account of Abraham in Genesis to show that faith was the instrument by which Abraham received the righteousness granted him by God (3:6). "Abram believed the LORD, and [H]e credited it to him as righteousness" (Genesis 15:6).

Abraham's faith was a robust faith, believing in the power of God in spite of his own sense of powerlessness because of his and Sarah's advanced age (Romans 4:19-21; Hebrews 11:11-12). He believed in the Lord and His promise in spite of the delay in the fulfillment of the promise (Acts 7:5; Hebrews 11:13), and in spite of not knowing what lay ahead in the future (Hebrews 11:8; Genesis 12:1).

Paul further uses a statement found several times in Genesis, "All nations will be blessed through you" (see 12:3; 18:18; 22:18; 26:4; 28:14) to show that the same principle of justification by faith applies to the Gentiles (Galatians 3:8). In fact, the statement was from its first appearance in Genesis intended to show that justification by faith applied to Gentile as well as Jewish believers. Abraham and his spiritual imitators, whether the Galatians or any believers that would follow in their train, have the same blessing through the same faith.

Experience of Habakkuk (3:11)

Lest his readers should think that he is being overly selective in examining the scriptural evidence, Paul adds the testimony of the prophets, this time from Habakkuk 2:4: "The righteous will live by his faith." This is the passage, through its citation by Paul in both Romans and Galatians, that was to have such an impact on Martin Luther and, through him, on a large segment of Christendom.

These words Paul would perhaps have understood in this context to mean, "Those who are righteous by faith will have life." In other words, "Receive God's provision of righteousness through faith, and you will receive eternal life." This interpretation of the quote would certainly fit the present context admirably and is not too great a strain on the passage's grammatical construction. If it is correct, it is completely in line with the quote from Genesis 15:6, which we have already examined. The way to righteousness is by faith.

These texts from Genesis and Habakkuk clearly demonstrate that the way of salvation is ever the same from dispensation to dispensation. There is not one way in the Old Testament and another in the New. Rather, all the people of God become such through faith in the divine word of promise. All who are truly God's people are the spiritual descendants of Abraham, the father of believers everywhere and throughout all time. (But we should be careful not to press the language to mean that there were no true believers before Abraham.[3])

Way of Works (Galatians 3:10-14)

Over against the true way to salvation through faith stands the way of salvation that the human mind finds all too attractive—the way of salvation by human effort. Although Paul's rejection of this way is implicit throughout the whole argument contained in the first half of chapter 3, it is dealt with in an explicit and concentrated way near the end of the section. This part is filled with allusions to the Old Testament Scriptures, especially the Pentateuchal books of Deuteronomy and Leviticus.

- Cursed is everyone who does not continue to do everything written in the Book of the Law (Galatians 3:10; see Deuteronomy 27:26).

- The man who does these things will live by them (Galatians 3:12; see Leviticus 18:5).

- Cursed is everyone who is hung on a tree (Galatians 3:13; see Deuteronomy 21:23).

At first this may appear to be little more than a string of quotes Paul has put together while engaged in the illegitimate exercise of proof texting. But on further reflection one may detect some rational development. The logic involved in the string of quotes seems to be somewhat as follows:

Law keeping is a matter of doing rather than believing (Galatians 3:12).

Furthermore, it is a matter of following *all* the law (completely and entirely) (3:10).

Those who fail in this endeavor stand under the law's curse (3:10).

Paul does not have to state what is obvious—namely, that all do in fact fail to keep the law perfectly—but this thought is certainly implied in his line of argumentation.[4]

The conclusion is inevitable: *all* are under the law's curse.

But Christ has rescued us from that curse by taking it upon Himself, and His crucifixion is evidence of this curse-bearing. From an Old Testament point of view, being hung on a tree or crucified on a cross would have been considered ample if not supreme evidence that one had been cursed (3:13).

The same thought of our being delivered from the curse is found in the verse that brings this section to a close: "He redeemed us in order that the blessing given to Abraham might come to the Gentiles through Christ Jesus, so that by faith we might receive the promise of the Spirit" (3:14). Here Paul seems to go further than his previous argument. He gathers together several strands of his thinking and identifies the blessing of justification by faith given to Abraham with the blessing of receiving the Spirit by faith.

Conclusion

As masterful as Paul's argumentation for his teaching may be, what really gives the doctrine its compelling power and spiritual appeal (in addition, of course, to the idea that it derives from the mind and mouth of God Himself) is the fact that it was born out of such deep personal experience. Paul, like Luther and countless others, had himself moved from a belief in salvation by works to the conviction that right standing with God was attained solely through simple trust in the perfect atoning work of the Lord Jesus Christ. And nowhere is this shift of perspective more clearly expressed than in his own testimony.

> If anyone else thinks he has reasons to put confidence in the flesh, I have more: circumcised on the eighth day, of the people of Israel, of the tribe of Benjamin, a Hebrew of Hebrews; in regard to the law, a Pharisee; as for zeal, persecuting the church; as for legalistic righteousness, faultless.
>
> But whatever was to my profit I now consider loss for the sake of Christ. What is more, I consider everything a loss compared to the surpassing greatness of knowing Christ Jesus my Lord, for whose sake I have lost all things. I consider them rubbish, that I may gain Christ and be found in him, not having a righteousness of my own, that comes from the law, but that which is through faith in Christ—the righteousness that comes from God and is by faith. (Philippians 3:4-9)

Paul, Luther—the list could go on and on, but perhaps a few more examples will suffice to show the doctrine of justification by faith not only as a firm teaching of God's Word but also as a living reality that transforms the human life.

What John Wesley described as his conversion experience followed a pattern similar to that of Paul and Luther. Although he had been a minister of the gospel for some years, he apparently came to the point where he felt that he had been carrying out that ministry in his own strength. Then came the experience of Wesley's attending a meeting where Luther's preface to his *Commentary on Romans* was being read. Listen to Wesley's own words as he describes this transforming moment.

> About a quarter before nine, while he was describing the change which God works in the heart through faith in Christ, I felt my heart strangely warmed. I felt I did trust in Christ, Christ alone, for salvation; and an assurance was given me, that He had taken away my sins, even mine, and saved me from the law of sin and death.[5]

Whether this was actually Wesley's conversion experience or one of his entering into an assurance of salvation, it still beautifully expresses the point for which Paul had so vigorously labored—the doctrine of justification by faith.

Over a thousand years earlier, the same sense of trusting in Christ came to Augustine. He had been struggling for some time with a lack of satisfaction in his own considerable achievements when he heard about some individuals who forsook their achievements and prospects to turn to a life of monastic living. From this context he envisioned Continence saying to him,

> Can you not do what these men and women do? Do you think they find strength to do it in themselves and not in the Lord their God? It was the Lord their God who gave me to them. Why do you try to stand in your

own strength and fail? Cast yourself upon Him without fear, for He will welcome you and take care of your ills.

Moments later Augustine was bidden to "take and read" the book upon which he had been meditating—Paul's epistle to the Romans—and this is what he read: "Arm yourselves with the Lord Jesus Christ." Augustine's response? "I had no wish to read more and no need to do so. For in an instant, as I came to the end of that sentence, it was as though the light of confidence flooded into my heart and all darkness was dispelled."[6]

Similar testimonies could be repeated over and over again.

Justification by faith. What a wonderful statement we find in this chapter concerning God's provision for sinful humanity! Both in its passion and in its logical argumentation this passage serves as a source of strength and assurance to any who are willing to admit personal sinfulness and turn to the Savior for restoration to a right standing with God.

> How vast the benefits divine
>   which we in Christ possess.
> We're saved from guilt and every sin
>   and called to holiness.
> It's not for works which we have done
>   or shall hereafter do,
> but He of His abounding love
>   salvation does bestow.
> The glory, Lord, from first to last,
>   is due to Thee alone.
> Aught to ourselves we dare not take
>   or rob Thee of Thy crown.[7]

Questions for Reflection or Discussion

1. How does Paul's calling the Galatians foolish (Galatians 3:1) relate to Christ's warning recorded in Matthew 5:22?
2. What are the implications in the word "portrayed" (Galatians 3:1)?
3. At what point in the Galatians' experience did they receive the Spirit (3:2), begin with the Spirit (3:3) and have the Spirit given to them (3:5)?
4. What is implied in Paul's saying that it was the Scripture (rather than God) that announced to Abraham, "All nations will be blessed through you" (3:8)?
5. How does 3:14 shed light on the announcement given to Abraham (3:8)?
6. What is the "blessing given to Abraham" (3:14)?

Endnotes

1. The language is capable of being understood in different ways. The idea is likely not that of coming to perfection thought of as a distinct, higher level of Christian experience. The NIV represents a minimalist interpretation with its "trying to attain your goal."
2. The verb *epathete* could have a more neutral meaning and be translated "you experienced." On the whole, however, it seems preferable to understand it in the sense of the Galatians' suffering persecution because of their reception of the gospel. Embracing the gospel regularly involved suffering persecution at the hands of unbelieving countrymen.
3. At least it is Hebrews' conviction in chapter 11 that true faith existed from the days of Abel. Compare the implicit attribution of faith to the time of Seth in Genesis 4:26.
4. The point will become explicit in 3:22.
5. *The Heart of John Wesley's Journal*, ed. Percy Livingstone Parker (New York: Fleming H. Revell Co., 1903), 43.
6. *Confessions*, trans. R.S. Pine-Coffin (Harmondsworth: Penguin Books Ltd., 1961), Book VIII, chapters 11-12.
7. Augustus M. Toplady, "How Vast the Benefits Divine" (a hymn).

The Continuity
of Paul's Gospel

Galatians 3:15-29

Brothers, let me take an example from everyday life. Just as no one can set aside or add to a human covenant that has been duly established, so it is in this case. The promises were spoken to Abraham and to his seed. The Scripture does not say "and to seeds," meaning many people, but "and to your seed," meaning one person, who is Christ. What I mean is this: The law, introduced 430 years later, does not set aside the covenant previously established by God and thus do away with the promise. For if the inheritance depends on the law, then it no longer depends on a promise; but God in his grace gave it to Abraham through a promise.

What, then, was the purpose of the law? It was added because of transgressions until the Seed to whom the promise referred had come. The law was put into effect through angels by a mediator. A mediator, however, does not represent just one party; but God is one.

Is the law, therefore, opposed to the promises of God? Absolutely not! For if a law had been given that could impart life, then righteousness would certainly have come by the law. But the Scripture declares that the whole world is a prisoner of sin, so that what

*was promised, being given through faith in Jesus Christ, might be
given to those who believe.*

*Before this faith came, we were held prisoners by the law, locked
up until faith should be revealed. So the law was put in charge to
lead us to Christ that we might be justified by faith. Now that faith
has come, we are no longer under the supervision of the law.*

*You are all sons of God through faith in Christ Jesus, for all of
you who were baptized into Christ have clothed yourselves with
Christ. There is neither Jew nor Greek, slave nor free, male nor female, for you are all one in Christ Jesus. If you belong to Christ,
then you are Abraham's seed, and heirs according to the promise.*

It is already clear that salvation is through faith, not through
works or keeping the law. But the law is such an integral part
of God's revelation in the Old Testament. What is its purpose?
How is it related to the divine revelation that preceded it—the
promise made to Abraham? And how does Paul's gospel relate
to the law and to the promise?

It is to these questions that Paul now turns in a rather lengthy
chain of argumentation extending from 3:15 to at least 4:7. In it
he seeks to establish that his gospel stands in continuity with
the promise made to Abraham and in some degree of disconti-
nuity with the law given through Moses. This long section can
be divided only artificially. Nevertheless, it is convenient to
separate a more general discussion of these relationships from
the more specific focus that becomes prominent in 4:1-7 but is
already anticipated in 3:22-25: namely, the particular function
of the law that may be described as tutelary or custodial. Here
we will focus on the Promise.[1]

"Promises, promises," we say rather cynically regarding potentially disappointing pledges made by humans. But the promises of the God who is Himself Absolute Truth are entirely
dependable. Although Paul would never exalt the promise of
God above the God who makes the promise, the promise itself
is still something very precious to him. That is at least partly be-

cause any promise that is going to be kept is such a precious possession to begin with.

Think for a moment of the promise that David made to Jonathan as a result of their intimate friendship. Jonathan requested that David never cut off his kindness to the family of Saul and Jonathan—not even when the Lord had cut off every one of David's enemies from the face of the earth—and David committed himself to that request by a covenant promise (1 Samuel 20:14-15, 42). Much later, in his time of power and authority, David remembered this promise: he spared Mephibosheth, son of Jonathan, the son of Saul, because of the oath before the Lord between Jonathan and himself (2 Samuel 9:7).

If promises on the human level have such authority and their fulfillment (if they are promises of good) brings such hope and comfort, how much more beloved are promises when they are the promises of the Almighty God! Those are the promises Paul has clearly in mind as he develops the thought of this section.

Sadly, not all human promises are of the kind illustrated above. In fact, human experience is full of broken promises. A memorable case in point is the way Adolf Hitler made and broke promise after promise in the course of events leading up to and during World War II.

In 1934 he promised not to invade Austria and then proceeded to break that promise in 1938 with his Anschluss invasion. He made a similar promise in 1935 not to invade Poland but broke his word by a brutal invasion in 1939. He promised in 1938 not to invade Czechoslovakia but then invaded it the very next year. And his promise not to invade Russia was made in 1939 and broken in 1941. Quite a record for the systematic breaking of publicly acknowledged promises!

Fortunately we can recall from the same general era the promise General Douglas MacArthur made to the Filipinos when he was driven from their islands that he would return to them, a promise he was able to keep at the end of the war. And even if he had been unable to keep that promise, it still would have been made in good faith, something that hardly could be said of the commitments Hitler had made.

None of this ambivalence is present, however, in the divine promises. His word stands sure. "What I have said, that will I bring about," says the Lord (Isaiah 46:11).

Based on this concept of the divine promise, Paul's argument seems here to take the following form: God's promise to Abraham was neither set aside by the law nor contradicted by it; rather, that promise continues to be in effect until this very day. On the other hand, it must be clearly understood that the promise of God does not find fulfillment in all of Abraham's descendants without distinction, but only in those who, like Abraham, are people of faith.

Promise Was Not Set Aside by Law (Galatians 3:15-18)

Paul argues that the promise God made to Abraham was not broken or set aside in any way. More particularly, it cannot be maintained that the Law given by God at Mt. Sinai somehow nullified the covenant promises God had previously so solemnly made. As he says in 3:17, "The law . . . does not set aside the covenant previously established by God and thus do away with the promise."

So the law, in spite of its God-ordained origin, should never, Paul maintains, be thought of as somehow a replacement for the promise, as if one way of God's dealing with sinful man had been set aside and another method brought in as a substitute mode of salvation. The law is a supplement to the promise, not a replacement for it.

Theoretically, the fact that the law came after the promise might be open to more than one interpretation. It might be argued, and perhaps was so argued by Paul's opponents, that its subsequent appearance is evidence of its superiority. Paul, however, takes a different approach, to the effect that what is prior is primary and what is subsequent is secondary. In fact, the law was not merely subsequent to the promise; it came a *long time* after the promise, to be specific, 430 years after it (3:17).[2] The superiority of the promise, based on its temporal priority, thus is clearly expressed in the text and is one of its major emphases.

Furthermore, Paul argues that a promise is by nature a gift graciously given. God was not compelled to make a promise to Abraham. Rather, it was spoken out of His grace (3:18). And law could in no way reverse that gift of grace, because for God to go back on His promise would be unthinkable.

Paul attempts to support his premise that the law, being later, did not set aside the promise by drawing on the analogy of the human institution of a last will and testament. Such a document, once it has been duly drawn up, cannot be revoked, he argues. Why, then, would it be any different with the divine promise?

Of course, implicit in the development of this argument is the connection between promise and covenant and between covenant and testament. But these connections are easily made, and once made, the logic of Paul's discussion becomes evident. Just as a human last will and testament cannot easily be nullified, so it is with God's testamental promise with Abraham. It cannot be thought of as being replaced by the Law.

It is interesting also to see how Paul in this way relates God's activity of promise-making to similar phenomena in the human arena. In this sense, God's activity is not something so totally other that it cannot be in any way related to human conceptualization. Rather, God's act can be understood by analogy to a human institution. God comes down to our level to help us understand His work.

In fact, the relationship between human institutions and the divine promise goes beyond the particular example Paul has drawn on—the practice of writing a last will and testament. Twentieth-century Old Testament scholarship has rather extensively developed the analogy between ancient Near Eastern treaties and God's covenant with Israel and with her forebears. God, it seems, is not averse to dealing with mankind in ways that can be understood in terms of human customs. Such is His condescension to our level in the course of salvation history.

Promise Was Not Opposed by Law (3:19-25)

Paul has argued that the promise is of primary importance, and so naturally the law has a secondary position. As such it could hardly set aside the provisions of the promise. But neither did it introduce an alternative way of salvation. It is not as if, once the law was introduced, there were now two ways for sinful humanity to relate to God—either through promise or through law. The answer to Paul's rhetorical question in 3:21, "Is the law, therefore, opposed to the promises of God?" is a resounding "Absolutely not!"

The law is related to the promise as something that is in a subordinate role. The law exists within the framework of the promise. The promise is not set aside by the law, but neither is it ruled out by the promise. Paul argues that the law, because of its subordinate nature, had a restricted purpose that by no means conflicted with the purpose of the promise. His argument is stated in verses that are filled with disputed points of interpretation. Nevertheless, we can detect some of Paul's concern with a degree of clarity.

First, the law was added (3:19). This further strengthens the idea that it was something supplementary and subordinate.

Secondly, it was added "because of transgressions." While there is no clear consensus as to what precisely this phrase means,[3] nevertheless, it again points to the fact that the law was in response to some existing condition. The law addresses a deficiency in the condition of those already under the Abrahamic promise. It does not, however, oppose the promise itself.

Of course, the promise too was concerned with the deficiency in mankind because of transgression. After all, as we have seen, the central element of the promise was the gift of God's righteousness, that is, justification. It is not that this justification was merely the *intent* of the promise and that this intent did not bring forth the desired effect. At the very least, it was effective in Abraham, who was actually counted righteous by God. So it is not as though the promise had failed and that God had brought in the law to do what the promise could not accomplish.

On the other hand, the promise did not emphasize the bad news regarding human sinfulness as the law could. The emphasis of the promise was on deliverance from transgression, that is, the provision of righteousness, rather than on the transgression itself. But with the law, it is just the other way around. The emphasis is on the transgression and its seriousness, but still allowing for the possibility of forgiveness through the grace of God.

Thirdly, the law's subordinate position within the framework of the promise is further indicated by its temporary character (3:19). It was in effect until the coming of the Seed, which is the coming of Christ. Presumably when that event was fulfilled, there would be no need for the law to continue to exist. But the promise would remain in effect. The promise is permanent. There is nothing that suggests any fundamental opposition between law and promise.

In the fourth place, the institution of the law through intermediate agencies is yet another testimony to its subordinate role. The fact that interpreters have a great deal of difficulty with the precise meaning of 3:20 does not at all render the overall sense of this statement incomprehensible. In contrast, the promise had been instituted directly by God (3:17), not through an intermediary.

Finally, the law's not being opposed to the promises of God is witnessed to by its inability to provide life and therefore righteousness (3:21). The result of this inability is, of course, the confinement of every human being to the prison of sin, so that we are driven to seek and find salvation from sin in another place, the way of faith in Jesus and His atoning work on our behalf (3:22). But that is to anticipate what will be more extensively discussed in the next chapter.

Actually, this last point concerning the law's inability to grant righteousness is at the heart of Paul's argumentation. Far from the law's providing an alternative method of salvation, it simply could not save. The law was powerless to accomplish for mankind what was needed—life and righteousness.

Promise Was Not Made Indiscriminately (3:26-29)

Although Paul's main thought is the idea that the law did not nullify or oppose the promise, there is another aspect to his argument that may profitably be raised and pondered. That is the question concerning the identity of the promise's recipient: to whom was the promise to Abraham actually made? This is no small matter to Paul, who clearly states already in 3:16, "The promises were spoken to Abraham and to his seed. The Scripture does not say 'and to seeds,' meaning many people, but 'and to your seed,' meaning one person, who is Christ." Paul is quite meticulous in his interpretation of the exact wording of his Genesis text and seems to belabor the point. But he has a point to make. The same concern with the recipient of the promise is present in 3:19, which more strictly says, "until the Seed to whom the promise *was made*[4] had come." Let us explore this issue more fully.

First, although Paul goes to great lengths to demonstrate the singularity of the seed, there are other aspects of the section that point to a corporate understanding. This is entirely appropriate for the interpretation of a noun that has not only singular and plural meaning, but also a collective sense. Paul's meaning is that the promises were not made to Abraham's descendants indiscriminately, but to Christ and those in Him.

Moreover, this collective or corporate understanding of Abraham's seed as embodied in the Messiah and His followers, although anticipated in 3:16, now becomes the main focus of 3:26-29, especially when Paul says, "If you belong to Christ, then you are Abraham's seed" (3:29). Here the concept of Abraham's seed is not only interpreted as plural; it is also given a Christocentric identity. It is only in Christ that we are the seed of Abraham.

In this passage the familiar Pauline phraseology expressing the thought of the union between Christ and the believer is found in such phrases as "baptized into Christ," "clothed . . . with Christ," "in Christ Jesus" and "belong[ing] to Christ." Through this identification with Christ the believer is part of the seed to whom the promises were made, the "corporate Christ."

Secondly, this concept of the believer's union with Christ has important practical consequences, for the believer is thereby united to every other believer in a Christian "brotherhood," in which the significance of certain common social distinctions of Paul's day is greatly reduced. We are all one in Christ (3:28), whether Jew or Greek, slave or free, male or female.

This important passage is not, however, to be understood as eradicating these distinctions in all possible relationships. Paul is careful to put the teaching in the context of an overall concern with our relationship to God, whereby we are made His children and His heirs. In terms of that relationship, there is no difference between Jew and Greek, slave and free, male and female. Thus this statement in 3:28 is in reality a comment on the word "all" in 3:26-28. You are all sons of God through faith

(3:26); all those baptized into Christ have clothed themselves with Christ (3:27); and you are all one in Christ (3:28).

Nonetheless, even on this rather cautious reading of 3:28, one can see its potential for providing a basis for a far-reaching sense of respect and appreciation for the value of each member of the body of Christ. In the body of Christ and in our spiritual relationship to Him, we are equals, not neglecting to keep in mind, however, the God-ordained ordering of officers or offices in the leadership of the church.[5]

Finally, it may be worth raising and exploring another possible application of the identity of the promise's recipient(s). We begin by noting that the only places in the book of Genesis where the precise Hebrew phrase "and to your seed" in conjunction with the promise is found are in 13:15 and 17:8, and that both of these either focus on or include God's promise of a land to inherit. In this connection it is also interesting that Paul begins in this section to use the category of inheritance (Galatians 3:18, 29) to describe the content of the promise. Without denying a spiritual dimension to this term, we may wonder whether there is not something here that assists us in our understanding of the complex issues concerning national rights to the land of Israel/Palestine today. Along with factors emphasizing longevity of a particular political or ethnic group's possession of the land or of their being lineally connected with Abraham, it may be that the most important idea is that the promise, including the land promise, is made to Christ. It is, then, fundamentally the Messiah's land, not Israel's or Ishmael's.

Conclusion

What a wonderful thing it is to be "in Christ." It is little wonder that Paul makes such significant use of the "in Christ" motif. Whether in that exact form ("in Christ") or couched in other terminology ("with Christ," "Christ in us," "clothed with Christ," "united with Christ," etc.), the teaching is surely fundamental in his thinking. Being in Christ is nothing short of being a Christian in the truest sense of the term. And that is something very wonderful indeed.

But beyond this, the concept of being in Christ or related to Christ provides the foundation for what has become known as the deeper life. Not just salvation but all of our blessings are in Christ—our wisdom, our righteousness and our holiness, as well as our redemption (1 Corinthians 1:30). Christ is the power of God and the wisdom of God (1:24). And it is according to that power that is at work within us that God is able to do immeasurably more than all we could ask or imagine (Ephesians 3:20). Truly, in Christ there is fullness of life. The Christian life—especially the deeper life—is the Christ-life. It is centered in Him.

Likewise, what a wonderful experience it is to receive a promise. But as wonderful as that experience is on the human level, how much more wonderful it is to receive the promises of God, who does not break—who cannot break—His promises. As the writer to the Hebrews says,

> Because God wanted to make the unchanging nature of his purpose very clear to the heirs of what was promised, he confirmed it with an oath. God did this so that, by two unchangeable things in which it is impossible for God to lie, we who have fled to take hold of the hope offered to us may be greatly encouraged. (Hebrews 6:17-18)

So the eternal God does not break His promises. Furthermore, the promises He has made to His children are exceeding great and precious ones, so great and so precious that through them we may be able to "participate in the divine nature and escape the corruption in the world caused by evil desires" (2 Peter 1:4).

There was a day when even human promises were held to be sacred, when people hardly dared to break them, no matter what the personal cost or effort involved. Sadly, such a day is no more, and promise after promise is treated as of no particular consequence. May this casual attitude to the integrity of a person's word not be found among the people of God. As James says, echoing the words of the Lord (Matthew 5:37), "Let your 'Yes' be yes, and your 'No,' no" (James 5:12).

> How large the promise, how divine, to Abram and his
>   seed:
> "I am a God to thee and thine, supplying all thy need."
>   The words of His unbounded love from age to age
>   endure.
>   The Covenant Angel still doth prove and seal the
>   blessing sure.
> Jesus the ancient faith confirms, to our great father
>   given.
> He takes His children to His arms and calls them heirs
>   of heaven.
>   O God, how faithful are Thy ways! Thy love
>   endures the same,
>   nor from the promise of Thy grace blots out Thy
>   children's name.[6]

Questions for Reflection or Discussion

1. Was Paul's statement in Galatians 3:15 literally true for his day, that no one could ever set aside or add to a human covenant that had been duly established? Could testaments be changed, revoked or supplemented by codicils?

2. What dates for Abraham and the giving of the law are implied in the 430 years (3:17)?

3. What motivated God's promise to Abraham (3:18)?

4. How does Paul's statement that God is one relate to the argument (3:20)?

5. When Paul says, *"if* a law had been given that could impart life" (3:21), what is he implying about the possibility of such a law?

6. Is it legitimate to distinguish between Abraham's seed (3:29) and Abraham's children (3:7)?

Endnotes

1. It is somewhat curious that the Old Testament does not refer to the Abrahamic promise as a promise, whereas it is such a main concern of Paul that it be analyzed as a promise. It has plausibly been suggested that the Old Testament was construed as a promise (*epangelia*) to correspond with the New Testament gospel (*euangelion*). See Gerhard Kittel, ed., *Theological Dictionary of the New Testament* (Grand Rapids: Eerdmans, 1964), II, 579.

2. The exact determination as to when the 430 years is thought to begin and end has always been problematic.

3. The preposition *charin* has a wide variety of meanings ranging from "for the sake of, on behalf of " to "on account of, because of."

4. Literally, "to whom it had been promised." It can be legitimately interpreted "to whom the promise had been made" but only very remotely "to whom the promise referred" (NIV).

5. First Timothy 2:12, for example, appears to put some limits on the principle of equality between the sexes.

6. Isaac Watts, "How Large the Promise, How Divine, to Abram and His Seed" (a hymn).

8

The Privileges of Paul's Gospel

Galatians 4:1-11

What I am saying is that as long as the heir is a child, he is no different from a slave, although he owns the whole estate. He is subject to guardians and trustees until the time set by his father. So also, when we were children, we were in slavery under the basic principles of the world. But when the time had fully come, God sent his Son, born of a woman, born under law, to redeem those under law, that we might receive the full rights of sons. Because you are sons, God sent the Spirit of his Son into our hearts, the Spirit who calls out, "Abba, Father." So you are no longer a slave, but a son; and since you are a son, God has made you also an heir.

Formerly, when you did not know God, you were slaves to those who by nature are not gods. But now that you know God—or rather are known by God—how is it that you are turning back to those weak and miserable principles? Do you wish to be enslaved by them all over again? You are observing special days and months and seasons and years! I fear for you, that somehow I have wasted my efforts on you.

Paul's discussion of the law has up to this point been largely negative, describing its secondary and temporary character. Now at last he turns to a further development of the law's specific purpose as tutor or custodian. This theme had already been alluded to briefly in 3:22-25, but it is not until 4:1-7 that it receives a fuller and definitive treatment. The subject is characterized by a number of key terms.

On the negative side Paul uses, among others, the terms "under" and "slavery." Thus we were

- held prisoners under the law (3:23, literal translation; NIV has "by the law")

- under the supervision of the law (3:25)

- under guardians and trustees (4:2, literal translation; NIV has "subject to")

- under law (4:5)

Likewise, we are described as being:

- no different from a slave (4:1)

- in slavery under the basic principles of the world (4:3)

- slave/slaves (4:7-8)

- enslaved by weak and miserable principles (4:9)

On the positive side he talks about our being redeemed (4:5) and treated as sons (4:5-7).

Using these and other categories, Paul draws a contrast between the conditions of the human race, or more particularly the people of God, before and after the coming of Christ. The turning point between the two "moments" in the history of God's people is called the fullness of time (4:4), the coming of faith (3:23, 25). The stage of maturity is referred to as "now" (4:9), and the anticipatory stage is indicated by "until" (3:23; 4:2) or "formerly" (4:8). Essentially, then, these two periods may be thought of as a state of bondage, followed by one of privilege.

In regard to the state of bondage, it can actually be viewed in four ways. First, it is presented under the figure of imprisonment, as in 3:23: "Before this faith came, we were held prisoners by the law, locked up until faith should be revealed."

A second way Paul describes it is as a period of supervision, using the analogy of the ancient institution of putting a person in charge of an immature child in a well-to-do family. "So the law was put in charge to lead us to Christ that we might be justified by faith. Now that faith has come, we are no longer under the supervision of the law" (3:24-25). "What I am saying is that as long as the heir is a child, he is no different from a slave, although he owns the whole estate. He is subject to guardians and trustees until the time set by his father" (4:1-2).

Furthermore, Paul sometimes uses the idea of slavery itself to express this condition of bondage. "So also, when we were children, we were in slavery under the basic principles of the world" (4:3).

Finally, the state of bondage can also be described as one of ignorance. "Formerly, when you did not know God, you were slaves to those who by nature are not gods" (4:8). This ignorance does not render us excusable before God. Rather, our ignorance is itself a result of willful rebellion against the Creator. As Paul says elsewhere, it is due to the hardening of our hearts (Ephesians 4:18).

We can easily see how fluid and overlapping these representations are and how naturally Paul blends them together in his description of the state of bondage without maintaining any rigid distinctions between the various terms.

What now needs to be addressed is the nature of that bondage. To what specifically were we held in bondage?

The most obvious answer to this is that our bondage is to the law (Galatians 3:23-25). Paul twice makes reference to bondage to the basic principles of the world, which he also calls weak and miserable (4:3, 9). But the most specific statement comes in his description in 4:10: "You are observing special days and months and seasons and years!"

When we put all these descriptions together, we can see that what Paul has in mind is the so-called ceremonial law of the Old Testament, some of which corresponds to analogous regulations in the world at large. This conclusion is strengthened when we recall that another part of the ceremonial law, circumcision, is also very much on Paul's mind in this letter.[1]

If this line of thinking can be accepted as an accurate assessment of Paul's ideas, we may conclude that his teaching can be summarized in the following way: It was necessary, in the divine purpose, for God to put His people temporarily under the supervisory guardianship of ritual and ceremonial laws, from which, in the fullness of time, they would be redeemed.

In contrast to the restrictions of bondage stand the privileges enunciated in Paul's gospel, which consist of the enjoyment of the full rights involved in the position of sonship, the presence of the Spirit and possession of the knowledge of God. In each case, however, the contrast between the privileges of the gospel and the previous state of bondage is not to be understood as an absolute one, but as only a relative difference between the two states. Consider briefly, then, these three marvelous privileges of the gospel age.

Position of Sonship (4:4-7)

While the privilege of being a child is universal, the enjoyment of that privilege is dependent on any number of factors.

These could include, among other things, the quality of the parenting, the age of the child, the nature of the relationship between parent and child and the external circumstances under which the relationship exists. All of these and more could affect the quality of the enjoyment of the childhood experience. But even in less than ideal situations, there is still an unrivaled uniqueness about being a child.

Take, for example, David's reaction to the death of his son Absalom, in what must surely be among the most poignant lines in all of Scripture: "O my son Absalom! My son, my son Absalom! If only I had died instead of you—O Absalom, my son, my son!" (2 Samuel 18:33).

It did not matter to King David at that moment that Absalom had been nearly successful in leading a rebellion against him. All that concerned him was that his son had died. Whatever else Absalom was, he was still David's son, still in that unique position of privilege.

It is that position of privilege that Paul now applies to the believer in Christ, and to do so, he uses this concept of sonship in a generic sense. We are certainly not to conclude that Paul, by using the masculine form of expression, was discriminating in any manner against female believers in Christ. In fact, if any writer in the Bible could go out of his way to expressly include women in the blessings of the gospel, it was Paul. That may come as something of a shock to those who have been encouraged to think of Paul as an archetypical male chauvinist. But this is also the Paul who can speak of the people of God as His sons *and daughters* (2 Corinthians 6:18),[2] where the Old Testament text he seems to be quoting has a reference only to God's sons. It is Paul's insight, or at the very least his willingness, to broaden the Old Testament text so as to be more inclusive.

The privileges entailed in this "sonship" are at least twofold: inheritance and intimacy, both of which are clearly thought of throughout the present context. Let us examine each of them briefly.

Inheritance

The concept of inheritance is never far from Paul's mind, being more or less continuously present in the apostle's thought from Galatians 3:29 ("you are Abraham's seed, and heirs according to the promise") to 4:7 ("since you are a son, God has made you also an heir"). It had already been used in 3:18 to designate the content of the Abrahamic promise: "For if the inheritance depends on the law, then it no longer depends on a promise; but God in his grace gave it to Abraham through a promise." Promise is the form; the inheritance is the content of the promise.

Even so, it is not immediately evident what constitutes the inheritance. It might be thought that the inheritance promised to Abraham is primarily the land God promised to him. And surely this is a dominant way of viewing the promise within the Old Testament itself. Nevertheless, there are dimensions of the promise given to Abraham that transcend the promise of land. We think, of course, of God's promise to be God to Abraham and to his seed (Genesis 17:7). It would seem that Paul is concentrating on that aspect of the promise in his remarks here in Galatians 3 and 4. The inheritance is primarily the blessing of justification by faith (3:14) and the gift of the Spirit (3:14, 4:6). In a very real sense, therefore, sonship is not simply something that entitles one to an inheritance; the position of sonship is itself part of the inheritance.

Intimacy

Sonship not only permits the child to inherit; it also allows intimacy. The intimacy comes to expression in this passage in the filial cry *"Abba,* Father," prompted in our hearts by the Spirit (4:6). It is open to question whether this filial cry is simply the recognition of and delight in God as our Father or whether it refers also to the petitions that may be introduced by such a form of address. If it is the latter, then implied in this aspect of sonship is the privilege of exercising intimacy with the Father by coming before Him and making known our requests. As Francis Lyall has said, "Participation in the family councils is of course but one of the privileges of sonship."[3]

Another intriguing privilege of sonship suggested by Lyall is the possession of the family property communally. While this aspect of the privilege of sonship is not as explicit in this section, it may still be there implicitly. This is especially a possibility in view of the corporate concerns expressed in the previous section, which, as we have argued, is very closely connected with the present one. Thus we are not only joint heirs with Christ; we are joint heirs with each other of the family inheritance.

Not only is sonship a privilege, but there are attendant duties as well. While these duties are not Paul's major concern in this passage, at least this much can be said: we cannot be individually sons of the father without seeking to maintain the unity of the family. We need to recognize and honor others in the family of God as equals before God (3:28), whatever their social or ethnic status.

It would not be right to conclude from this application of sonship to the Christian believer that believing Israelites were in no sense sons of God, for Deuteronomy 14:1 clearly states that they were. Rather, we must hold that, although God's Old Testament people were both collectively and individually His sons and daughters, yet they could not enjoy to the full their status of sonship because of the restrictive function of the ceremonial law. Now that those restrictions have been removed, says Paul, God's people can enjoy their full rights as sons. The contrast is thus a relative one, and this conclusion is completely in line with the analogy of the patrician child during his minority, who is still a son although he cannot exercise the rights of his sonship until the proper time (Galatians 4:1-2). It is a sonship experienced in immaturity, to be sure, but it is a degree of sonship.

Presence of the Spirit (4:6)

Very closely connected with the position of sonship is the second privilege of the believer in the fullness of time—that of possessing and enjoying the ministry of the Holy Spirit in a measure not available under the older dispensation. But once again we must insist that the difference between the experience of the Spirit in the older dispensation and that in the newer age is only a relative difference. Occasionally even in the Old Testament there are statements about the Spirit's ministry to the individual believer that come very close to descriptions of His ministry found in reference to the New Testament believer.

For example, while often the Spirit of God is spoken of as equipping certain kinds of people for ministry, sometimes only for brief and temporary periods, there are also indications that the Old Testament believer received the Spirit's ministries that are in the New Testament associated with regeneration, renewal, moral guidance and the like. Consider what the psalmist prays: "Teach me to do your will, for you are my God; may your good Spirit lead me on level ground" (Psalm 143:10).[4] Thus some of the Old Testament faithful experienced, or at least prayed to experience and apparently thought they could experience, the presence of God's Holy Spirit in their lives as an influence for moral direction and not simply as an equipping for specific service.

On the other hand, there does seem to be some difference between the experience of the Spirit by an Old Testament believer and that by the New Testament believer, but the difference is often difficult to specify in detail. Certainly one aspect of the difference lies in the fact that, after the coming of the Messiah, believers experience a Spirit who had by then already been experienced by the Messiah Himself as God-man. As John records, surely referring to Christ, "For the one whom God has sent speaks the words of God, for God gives the Spirit without limit" (John 3:34). Thus the Son receives the Spirit in unmeasured degree. Then out of His own personal possession and experience of the Spirit, He Himself can receive the promised Holy Spirit and pour it out (Acts 2:33. See also John 1:16). That is why Paul can refer to the Spirit here as the Spirit of God's Son (Galatians 4:6). It is the Messiah's Spirit, the Messianic Spirit.

Possession of Knowledge (4:8-9)

The third privilege that Paul emphasizes is the privilege of knowing God. Again it seems obvious that the contrast with the former condition of ignorance is only relative. Surely the intended outcome of God's revealing Himself in Old Testament times is not ignorance but the experience of knowing Him, a point that we can see in the example of Moses' prayer: "Teach me your ways so I may know you" (Exodus 33:13).

It is also true that there is a strong emphasis in the Old Testament anticipating a knowledge of God in the future experience of God's people. The classic passages expressing this idea are in Jeremiah and Ezekiel. Jeremiah anticipates the day when "no longer will a man teach his neighbor, or a man his brother, saying, 'Know the LORD,' because they will all know me, from the least of them to the greatest" (Jeremiah 31:34). But the point of this implied contrast with Jeremiah's present surroundings is not that the anticipated knowledge of God will be a different kind of knowledge or even a different depth of knowing God. Rather, the new element is simply a more extensive and widespread knowledge of God throughout His people.

Actually, in this important passage in Jeremiah, to know God is very close to, if not identical with, the thought of acknowledging Him, confessing Him as God. It was Israel's persistent failing that they did not acknowledge Jehovah consistently and from the heart. But Jeremiah announces the day in which they will so acknowledge Him.

Of course, there were always some in the Old Testament period who did acknowledge Jehovah as God. There was always a remnant who did not bow the knee to Baal (1 Kings 19:18; Romans 11:4). But they were a relative few compared with what God would do for His people in the future events announced by Jeremiah.

Moreover, in other passages in Jeremiah, the knowledge of God has very practical consequences, if indeed these consequences are not a definition of such knowledge. Thus in Jeremiah 9:24, to know God is to know that He is "the LORD, who exercises kindness, justice and righteousness on earth, for in these [He] delights." Similarly, in Jeremiah 22:15-16, in a passage apparently extolling King Josiah, we find, "He did what was right and just. . . . He defended the cause of the poor and needy . . . . Is that not what it means to know me?" Knowing God cannot be separated from how we are to live.

Nor is the contrast between the old order and the new a contrast between a knowledge about God and a direct and personal knowledge of God Himself. In other words, there is no contrast between "knowledge that" (knowledge of facts) and "knowledge of" (knowledge of persons). That frequently made distinction is one that probably cannot be sustained. What some people take to be a qualitative difference is really only a quantitative difference. That is, the knowledge that a brother, for example, has of his illustrious sister differs from the knowledge that a scholar has of her only in the sense that the items that he knows about her are different. They are still facts that are known, just different facts;[5] still "knowledge about," not some different "knowledge of." In short, "knowledge of" reduces to "knowledge that."

The same distinction between what is perceived to be merely scholastic knowledge and the knowledge of intimacy is sometimes also detected in John 15:15, in its contrast between servants and friends. But here again this approach is a misreading of the facts of the passage. The contrast between servants and friends is a contrast between no knowledge and knowledge, or perhaps more accurately stated, between little knowledge and greater knowledge, not one between two qualitatively different kinds of knowledge.

Nevertheless, to argue, as we have done, that knowledge is basically knowledge of facts is not in the least intended to demean such knowledge. Rather, it is the glory of the gospel age to have access to a more extensive understanding of God's truth. And, of course, any extensive understanding we do have is not of our own doing or through our own ingenuity. On the contrary, the fuller knowledge of God the believer experiences in the fullness of time is granted by God's revealing Himself more fully. It is a corollary of progressive revelation.

Moreover, Paul does not pass up the opportunity to remind the Galatians that even more fundamental than the privilege of knowing God is the privilege of being known by God, which for Paul refers to God's sovereign election of the believer to this privileged status. In this sense, the knowledge that God has of His people is also more than bare knowledge. It is elective knowledge, elective love.

Conclusion

Position of Sonship, Presence of the Spirit, Possession of Knowledge—three of the most precious privileges of the believer. It is difficult, if not impossible, to say that one of them is more basic than another. Nevertheless, let us focus once more on the sonship theme.

It is interesting to observe how frequently in Scripture and in life the wonderful privileges of sonship are ignored, that instead of having intimacy and harmony between father and son, there are discord, strife and rebellion. This is born out, amazingly, in three consecutive generations of Old Testament leaders. Eli's sons were considerably less than ideal (1 Samuel 2). Then, instead of learning from the situation he witnessed, Samuel did no better with his sons (1 Samuel 8:1-3). Nor did David with his (2 Samuel 13–15). Sadly, the pattern is too often repeated.[6]

On the other hand, it is a joy to witness a father-son relationship that really does seem to approach the ideal. One example of this kind of situation is the Hodge family of the older Princeton Theological Seminary. We are thinking of Charles Hodge, the father and professor of systematic theology, and of his two sons, Archibald and Caspar, both of whom followed him in teaching responsibilities at the seminary.

Charles Hodge was one of the giants in nineteenth-century American evangelical Christianity, tirelessly defending the Scriptures against the growing influences of German rationalistic criticism and the Darwinian theory of evolution. Were it not for him, or someone like him in intellectual stature and piety, fidelity to the Bible would surely have declined in this country far more rapidly than it did.

His eldest son, Archibald Alexander Hodge, was particularly close to his father, both in his chosen field of systematics, the common theological perspective they shared, and in the mutual respect they held toward one another.[7] The son's respect for his father's scholarly ideals and the father's pride in his son's achievement are well illustrated in an anecdote recalled by Dr. Francis L. Patton at the time of the younger Hodge's death:

> On one occasion he won a compliment from his father which he must have valued highly, for he has told me the story more than once. It seems that he had written an essay, and on reading it to Dr. Charles Hodge, that distinguished theologian looked up with an expression of pleased astonishment on his face, and said that Alexander must read the essay to the class.[8]

Theirs was a father-son relationship at its best.

One of our Lord's most beloved parables (Luke 15:11-32) spoke about two sons, sons that were very different in the way they treated their sonship. The prodigal son abused his sonship in one way—through flagrant disregard of his father's wishes and in irresponsible squandering of his filial inheritance through riotous living. But from the father's perspective and in reality, he was still a son. The son himself knew he was not deserving of this status. Nevertheless, to the father he was always a son and through the father's love came to enjoy the status of sonship once again.

The elder son depreciated the position of sonship in a different way. He refused to see it as involving love and intimacy. And yet he was no less the son of the father. All that the father had was his, and no doubt he enjoyed at least the material substance resulting from his position of sonship. Even after the elder son's reaction to his father's kind treatment of the younger brother, he could have gone on to find enjoyment of his sonship in a deeper way. But apparently he chose not to pursue it.

Of these two, the one who most closely entered into the kind of mature sonship Paul was talking about in Galatians was the younger son, the prodigal—not, of course, because he had been a prodigal son, but because he was willing to come to the father in obedience and trust completely and solely in the father's love. His was a sonship born out of faith and resulting in intimacy. That is the kind of sonship we find in Galatians.

God invites us to intimacy with Himself. And there is no substantial reason why this intimacy may not grow deeper and deeper. It is indeed at the very heart of the deeper life.

> My Father God—that gracious sound dispels my
>   guilty fear.
> Not all the harmony of heaven could so delight my
>   ear.
>   Come, Holy Spirit, seal the grace on my expanding
>   heart,
>   And show that in the Father's love I share a filial
>   part.
> Cheered by a witness so divine, unwavering I believe,
> And "Abba Father" humbly cry, nor can the sign
>   deceive.[9]

Questions for Reflection or Discussion

1. What age would be referred to in "the time set by his father" (Galatians 4:2)?

2. Who are referred to in "those under law" (4:5)?

3. What is implied in saying that it is the Spirit that calls out, "*Abba,* Father" (4:6)?

4. What are "those who by nature are not gods" (4:8)?

5. Did Paul include the Sabbath in the special days to which the Galatians would be enslaved (4:10)? Why or why not?

6. What are the various ways in which Paul refers to the state of bondage in 3:22-25 and 4:1-11?

Endnotes

1. Paul treats this aspect of the matter extensively in chapter 5.
2. Scholarship sees Paul quoting from Second Samuel 7:14 based on the similarity in grammatical structure between the two passages, even though there are obvious differences as well. See Ralph P. Martin, *2 Corinthians* (Waco, TX: Word Books, 1986), 206-207. Paul may have been influenced by other Old Testament passages in which "daughters" is explicit (Isaiah 43:6). Paul is either injecting the addition of "daughters" or, at the very least, selecting the word from the Old Testament and conflating it with the primary passage being quoted. Either way, he cannot be charged at this point with blatant chauvinism.
3. Francis Lyall, *Slaves, Citizens, Sons: Legal Metaphors in the Epistles* (Grand Rapids: Zondervan, 1984), 122.
4. In the context of wanting to do God's will, this petition should be seen as the desire for moral and spiritual direction, not just physical protection.
5. Even if one holds that there are different kinds of items that are respectively known, they are still items (facts) about the person that are known, not the person independent of facts about the person.
6. It can only be something of an embarrassment that Dr. Simpson's sons did not turn out better than they did.
7. David B. Calhoun, *Princeton Seminary: Volume Two, The Majestic Testimony, 1869-1929* (Edinburgh: Banner of Truth Trust, 1996), 47-62.
8. A.A. Hodge, quoting Patton's Memorial Discourse in *Evangelical Theology: A Course of Popular Lectures* (Edinburgh: Banner of Truth Trust, [1890] 1976), xiii. (Dr. Patton, incidentally, was a classmate of Dr. A.B. Simpson at Knox College.)
9. Philip Doddridge, "Sovereign of All the Worlds on High" (a hymn).

The Fervency of Paul's Gospel

Galatians 4:12-31

I plead with you, brothers, become like me, for I became like you. You have done me no wrong. As you know, it was because of an illness that I first preached the gospel to you. Even though my illness was a trial to you, you did not treat me with contempt or scorn. Instead, you welcomed me as if I were an angel of God, as if I were Christ Jesus himself. What has happened to all your joy? I can testify that, if you could have done so, you would have torn out your eyes and given them to me. Have I now become your enemy by telling you the truth?

Those people are zealous to win you over, but for no good. What they want is to alienate you from us, so that you may be zealous for them. It is fine to be zealous, provided the purpose is good, and to be so always and not just when I am with you. My dear children, for whom I am again in the pains of childbirth until Christ is formed in you, how I wish I could be with you now and change my tone, because I am perplexed about you!

Tell me, you who want to be under the law, are you not aware of what the law says? For it is written that Abraham had two sons, one by the slave woman and the other by the free woman. His son by the slave woman was born in the ordinary way; but his son by the free woman was born as the result of a promise.

These things may be taken figuratively, for the women represent two covenants. One covenant is from Mount Sinai and bears children who are to be slaves: This is Hagar. Now Hagar stands for Mount Sinai in Arabia and corresponds to the present city of Jerusalem, because she is in slavery with her children. But the Jerusalem that is above is free, and she is our mother. For it is written:

> *"Be glad, O barren woman,*
> *who bears no children;*
> *break forth and cry aloud,*
> *you who have no labor pains;*
> *because more are the children of the desolate woman*
> *than of her who has a husband."*

Now you, brothers, like Isaac, are children of promise. At that time the son born in the ordinary way persecuted the son born by the power of the Spirit. It is the same now. But what does the Scripture say? "Get rid of the slave woman and her son, for the slave woman's son will never share in the inheritance with the free woman's son." Therefore, brothers, we are not children of the slave woman, but of the free woman.

B y this stage in the letter, Paul has made most of his theoretical argument and turns the discussion to a more practical emphasis, fervently dwelling on the seriousness of the issue facing the Galatians. Of course the gravity of the Galatians' situation had never been far from his thought, as we saw by his earlier expressions in chapter 1 ("I am astonished") and chapter 3 ("You foolish Galatians").

But at this point his concern for them breaks forth in an impassioned and fervent appeal, as shown in his use of words and phrases like "I plead with you" (4:12), "my dear children" (4:19), and "how I wish" (4:20). How can they even think of turning their back on Christ? Do they realize the seriousness of the compromise involved in following the new teaching that has come into their midst? What can now be done to deliver them from the erroneous teachings? Thus Paul pleads with them and tries to shock them into coming to their senses and finding their rest and salvation in Christ and Christ alone.

The appeal is based on a number of factors that they would be aware of from their own experience of receiving the gospel, and then further supported by a somewhat strange kind of scriptural argument, different from any that has been used up to this point.

Fervency Modeled by the One Ministering (4:12-13)

A minister of the gospel who does not hold fervency in ministry as an ideal is almost a contradiction in terms. Certainly such a fervent approach to ministry was characteristic of the great apostle. Paul first of all appeals to the Galatians on the basis of his own ministry among them, and it is an impassioned appeal indeed.

The fact that Paul had initially reached out to the Galatians ("I became like you") now provides a motive for them to respond to his urgent appeal that they return to the basics of his gospel message ("become like me"). His own fervent presentation of the gospel to them should now be reflected in their equally fervent response in embracing it once again.

Further, if his ministry among them had been because of an illness (4:13), it must also have been in spite of that illness. He apparently had been willing to set aside personal comfort in order to evangelize these Gentile communities that were unreached with the gospel. It is not necessary for us to know precisely what kind of illness Paul is referring to. It only matters that he labored among the Galatians under personally difficult physical circumstances.

Clearly Paul had inconvenienced himself to minister the gospel to them. Now he asks that they put forth a similar effort in return to embrace his ministry and the message of the gospel for which he had worked.

Fervency Encouraged by the Hearers' Response (4:14-16)

Next Paul appeals to the Galatians' initial reception of the gospel. Their original fervency in responding to the gospel should stimulate them now to a sincere return to their former spirit. Not only should their past acceptance of Paul's message form the basis of a present favorable attitude on *their* part toward his teaching, but it also encourages Paul to be fervent toward them. He rejoices in the Galatians' conversion experience and hopes they will recall it with the same spirit of rejoicing he feels.

There could hardly have been a more favorable response to the preaching of the gospel than that which the Galatians had made. At that time they welcomed him as if he were an angel sent from God, and would have been willing, he says, to tear out their eyes and give them to him, if that were possible. They had been willing not only to bear patiently with whatever illness he had labored under, but they had evidently done so without diminishing their respect for him (4:14). To them the external factors of outward appearance, style and circumstances were not as crucial as the humble, generous, fervent spirit which Paul had manifested in the course of ministering. Nor were they nearly as important as the essence of the gospel message itself. And that message they had gladly accepted in spite of any perceptible or imagined exterior deficiencies in the messenger.

With that kind of attitude in the background of their experience, they should now, says Paul, just return to that spirit and have confidence in their spiritual mentor at this present moment, as they had so readily and enthusiastically believed in him when he was with them at the time of their conversion.

Fervency Demanded by False Teaching (4:17-18)

The entrance, in the meantime, of others with a different teaching would be no problem if the teaching were really the true gospel; but it was not. So Paul calls on the Galatians to assess the interloping ministers and their dangerous doctrines in a realistic manner.

One way to test the legitimacy of a proclamation is to test for its correspondence to the facts. Naturally, the Galatians would have no way of testing Paul's gospel against the facts it purported to describe. Those events—the life, teachings, crucifixion and resurrection of the Messiah—were not directly accessible to the Galatians, and they would have to rely on less direct lines of authenticating the message they heard. Thus they needed to assess the message in other terms: in regard to its consistency, for example, or the apparent competence and reliability of its proclaimers. And there was no reason for faulting Paul's message on the basis that it did not authentically relate the gospel facts.

The same principles would be valid as well for testing for the truth or error of the false teachers. Were they competent? How plausible was their message? Surely they had no more definitive direct access to the original gospel events than Paul had. Then why should their version of the gospel be preferred over Paul's? Let the Galatians apply the same tests to both "gospels" equally, and it will be apparent that Paul's message is in no way inferior to that of his opponents.

But certainly another relevant factor would be the motivation of those proclaiming the message. Thus Paul exhorts the Galatians to examine the motives of those who had come to them with this different "gospel" message. And when their motives are subjected to careful examination, it will easily be seen that those motives are found to be wanting. They are self-centered.

The seriousness of the threat posed by the false teaching is another factor that fuels Paul's own fervency in his pleading with the Galatians. It should also inspire fervency within them as well.

Fervency Born out of Pastoral Concern (4:19-20)

Paul then introduces an intriguing analogy relating to the processes leading up to birth, employing the imagery of pregnancy and labor in childbirth to express his present pastoral concern for his readers. The main point of his words seems to be that he is experiencing spiritually the agony of birth pangs as he awaits their "rebirth" in the things of Christ.

Paul does not appear to pursue the analogy with strict logical consistency, however. The major tension is found in the fact that, on the one hand, it is Paul who is travailing in childbirth, and on the other hand, it is in the womb of the Galatians that Christ is developing or being formed. There is further tension between Paul's laboring in childbirth and the climactic moment at the end of that process being not birth but formation, presumably a reference to the developing embryo.

But setting aside such technical irregularities, we still must face the anomaly of Paul speaking about Christ's formation in the Galatians where we might have expected him to have alluded to the Galatians' formation in Christ.

Yet are the two really that different? That is, are they not simply two perspectives concerning the same basic reality? Do we not have similar mixing of metaphors in other attempts to describe the union of Christ and the believer? If we take this approach, the tensions involved in the imagery are somewhat relieved, and the passage then becomes significant for the concept of "spiritual formation." But even so, things are far from clear. Does the formation of Christ in the Galatians refer to their true conversion, to their return to the principles of the gospel, to the progressive development of the life of Christ in them or perhaps to the final moment of sanctification at the Second Coming of Christ?[1]

Among these various interpretive alternatives it may be difficult to choose, but we would not be on weak ground if we stressed the third—that Paul longed for their spiritual growth in Christ. Naturally, this option relates the passage most directly to the concept of the deeper life, the formation of Christ in the believer.

This connection with the deeper life, especially thought of as involving a progressive development of the Christ-life in the believer, would be strengthened if the present passage can be linked with Second Corinthians 3:18. There believers are said to be progressively transformed into the likeness of the Lord. The resemblance between "transformed" (2 Corinthians) and "formed" (Galatians) might establish a connection in thought between the two passages. If so, Paul's thought in Galatians may well be that of the spiritual formation of Christ in the life of the believer. On the other hand, the difference between *believers* being transformed and *Christ* being formed may militate against seeing an association between the two passages. Nevertheless, it still remains an attractive connection.

The use of the entire set of metaphors in this context raises once again the issue of the exact spiritual status of the Galatians: has Christ been formed in them or not? Has He been born in them or not? Perhaps the best understanding is that in which Paul assumes their genuine spiritual birth (after all, he does call them "brothers" in Galatians 4:12) but sees great deficiency in the way their life in Christ and Christ's life in them have proceeded. Like a true pastor, Paul fervently yearns for the Galatians' spiritual development.

Fervency Based on Scriptural Precedent (4:21-31)

Finally, Paul makes his appeal to the Galatians on the basis of Scripture. The Scripture Paul selects for application to the Galatian problem is from the life of Abraham, specifically the contrast between Ishmael and Isaac and especially the difference in the circumstances surrounding their respective births. Ishmael was conceived and born in a purely natural way through a slave woman, Hagar, who was less than a full wife in status. Isaac, on the other hand, was conceived apparently through special divine intervention, and was the son of Abraham's wife Sarah. Paul goes on to interpret these facts as indicating two kinds of people: children of bondage and those of liberty. And he naturally claims that the true believer is a child of God's bountiful gift of freedom and liberty in Christ.

It is clear that in the Galatians' set of circumstances, the words about slavery and bondage are applied to those who are still committed to Judaism ("Jerusalem") and who have Judaized the gospel of Christ. They are the "spiritual" descendants of Hagar through Ishmael and are still trapped in a system that can offer only spiritual slavery.

On the other hand, Paul takes the words about freedom to apply to the true follower of Christ. See how he develops the various aspects of this grand heritage as he unfolds the truths not only of their liberty in Christ, but also many other aspects of their position as well.

Christians are first of all children of freedom (4:26); they have been set free in Christ from the restrictive bondage of the Old Testament ceremonial laws. This simply restates and reinforces the teaching Paul had given earlier in chapters 3 and 4.

Secondly, they are children of heaven (4:26); they belong ultimately to another realm of existence, wherein is their true citizenship (Philippians 3:20). They are in the world but not of it (John 17:14-16). They are pilgrims seeking a heavenly city

(Hebrews 11:10, 13-16). The Jerusalem above is their true mother.

Thirdly, they are children of joy (Galatians 4:27). In the course of Paul's description of the children of liberty he draws on another passage, this time from the prophets (Isaiah 54:1), to show how the fortunes of God's people are turned from sadness to joy. Like Sarah, who was long barren and slow to produce an heir for Abraham, so the small nucleus of true believers in Galatia might seem overwhelmed by the apparently dominant Judaizing majority. But also like Sarah (and like the nation of Judah at a later period, of whom Isaiah was speaking), the tables will be turned and the desolate minority will come to rejoice in its spiritual heritage. The true believer, says Paul, participates in this joyous heritage.

In the fourth place, they are children of promise (Galatians 4:28); they have been established as God's people by His gracious will and promise, rather than coming into existence in any natural or ordinary fashion. Furthermore, they are destined not only to possess the promises but also eventually to receive the provisions that are promised.

Then, they are children of the Spirit (4:29). They are truly born by the power of the Spirit and sustained by the Spirit. And, as we will see in chapter 5, they live in the Spirit.

Next, they are children of persecution (4:29),[2] to which they are at the present time subject, if not physically, at least emotionally and spiritually. Paul elsewhere implies that a Christian's suffering persecution is to be expected (Acts 14:22; Philippians 1:29; 1 Thessalonians 3:3-4; 2 Timothy 3:12). But in spite of the present experience of persecution, they are also children destined to receive an inheritance (Galatians 4:30).

Finally—and this is the main point that Paul has been leading up to—we may also say that they are children of authority (4:30). They have the authority under God to deal with their persecutors—to cast them out. Despite the present hostility, the children of the promise and of the inheritance are also children possessing such authority. Sarah and by implication her son Isaac had the God-given authority to expel the slave woman and her son (Genesis 21:10-12). And so, in this regard, Paul cannot resist hinting at the obvious application for the current crisis in Galatia. Yet the point is too direct to need explanation: Get rid of the false teachers and their followers!

Conclusion

This passage fairly bristles with the note of gravity, of urgency—of fervency. We see Paul manifesting these concerns again and again in a concentrated effort to move the Galatians back to their first love.

But of course Paul was by no means the first to be fervent in ministry. Think of the Old Testament prophet Hosea. Out of a life of personal emotional suffering, he was well fitted to speak the agonizingly heartfelt appeal to Israel on behalf of his God (Hosea 11:1-4, 8).

> When Israel was a child, I loved him,
>   and out of Egypt I called my son.
> But the more I called Israel,
>   the further they went from me. . . .
> It was I who taught Ephraim to walk,
>   taking them by the arms;
> but they did not realize
>   it was I who healed them.
> I led them with cords of human kindness,
>   with ties of love;
> I lifted the yoke from their neck
>   and bent down to feed them. . . .
> How can I give you up, Ephraim?
>   How can I hand you over, Israel?

How can I treat you like Admah?
How can I make you like Zeboiim?

The same kind of heart-rending cry is also heard on the lips of the prophet Ezekiel (18:31-32): "Why will you die, O house of Israel? For I take no pleasure in the death of anyone, declares the Sovereign LORD. Repent and live!"

Moreover, we recall the similar fervency of the Lord Himself, as He wept over Jerusalem: "O Jerusalem, Jerusalem, you who kill the prophets and stone those sent to you, how often I have longed to gather your children together, as a hen gathers her chicks under her wings, but you were not willing" (Matthew 23:37).

So Paul was simply following in a long tradition of displaying a fervent compassion toward a spiritually needy audience. Nor would he be the last to do so. Even in his own day, his contemporary, Apollos, is portrayed by Luke as speaking "with great fervor" (Acts 18:25).

What is true of the great leaders should likewise be true of Christians generally. Thus Paul commends the Corinthian believers for their ardent concern for him (2 Corinthians 7:7) and exhorts the Roman saints never to be "lacking in zeal, but keep your spiritual fervor, serving the Lord" (Romans 12:11). In the same vein, Peter encourages his readers to love each other *deeply* (1 Peter 1:22).

May we too have the fervency of Paul in the proclamation of the gospel. May his words recorded elsewhere (2 Corinthians 5:20) be fulfilled in us: "We are therefore Christ's ambassadors, as though God were making his *appeal* through us. We *implore*[3] on Christ's behalf: Be reconciled to God" (emphasis mine).

Go, labor on. Spend and be spent,
Thy joy to do the Father's will.

It is the way the Master went.
  Should not the servant tread it still?

Go, labor on. 'Tis not for naught.
  Thy earthly loss is heavenly gain.
Men heed thee, love thee, praise thee not.
  The Master praises—what are men?

Go, labor on. Your hands are weak,
  Your knees are faint, your soul cast down.
Yet falter not. The prize you seek is near—
  A kingdom and a crown.

Go, labor on while it is day.
  The world's dark night is hastening on.
Speed, speed thy work. Cast sloth away.
  It is not thus that souls are won.

Toil on, faint not, keep watch and pray.
  Be wise the erring soul to win.
Go forth into the world's highway.
  Compel the wanderer to come in.

Toil on and in thy toil rejoice.
  For toil comes rest, for exile home.
Soon shalt thou hear the Bridegroom's voice,
  The midnight cry, "Behold I come."[4]

Questions for Reflection or Discussion

1. What does Paul mean by "like me" (Galatians 4:12)?
2. In what sense did Paul mean that "it is fine to be zealous" (4:18)?
3. Paul appears to have a different meaning in mind for each time he uses the word "law" in 4:21. What is he referring to in each case?

4. Does Paul deny a literal meaning to the Old Testament narrative when he says, "These things may be taken figuratively" (4:24)?

5. Is there a difference between "stands for" and "corresponds to" (4:25)? Does this wording imply two levels of figurative interpretation, or can the two expressions be reduced to one?

6. What is meant by "Mount Sinai in Arabia" (4:25)?

7. In what way are we like Isaac (4:28)?

Endnotes

1. The fact that the verb form is aorist does not automatically rule out any of these possibilities, although some would see it as at least slightly favoring any but the third. The aorist tense can be harmonized with the third (progressive sanctification) if it is seen as global rather than as indicating a narrow point in time.

2. The nature of the persecution in Genesis 21:9-12 is not entirely clear, but it may have had a particularly sinister tone.

3. The word "you" is not in the Greek.

4. Horatius Bonar, "Go, Labor On" (a hymn).

10

The Liberty of Paul's Gospel

Galatians 5:1-15

It is for freedom that Christ has set us free. Stand firm, then, and do not let yourselves be burdened again by a yoke of slavery.

Mark my words! I, Paul, tell you that if you let yourselves be circumcised, Christ will be of no value to you at all. Again I declare to every man who lets himself be circumcised that he is obligated to obey the whole law. You who are trying to be justified by law have been alienated from Christ; you have fallen away from grace. But by faith we eagerly await through the Spirit the righteousness for which we hope. For in Christ Jesus neither circumcision nor uncircumcision has any value. The only thing that counts is faith expressing itself through love.

You were running a good race. Who cut in on you and kept you from obeying the truth? That kind of persuasion does not come from the one who calls you. "A little yeast works through the whole batch of dough." I am confident in the Lord that you will take no other view. The one who is throwing you into confusion will pay the penalty, whoever he may be. Brothers, if I am still preaching circumcision, why am I still being persecuted? In that case the offense of the cross has been abolished. As for those agitators, I wish they would go the whole way and emasculate themselves!

You, my brothers, were called to be free. But do not use your freedom to indulge the sinful nature; rather, serve one another in

133

> *love. The entire law is summed up in a single command: "Love*
> *your neighbor as yourself." If you keep on biting and devouring*
> *each other, watch out or you will be destroyed by each other.*

The freedom of the believer in Christ has already been established in the previous section of the letter. But what does
that freedom mean in practice? How far does Christian liberty
extend? What are its limits, if any?

On the one hand, there have been those who have failed to
appreciate their God-given Christian freedom in any meaningful sense. These benighted folk approach their Christian faith
so legalistically that they can only be seen from a more bal-
anced perspective as essentially denying any genuine Christian
liberty.

Then there are those, on the other hand, who interpret their
Christian freedom so radically that they appear to be bound by
little in the way of concrete moral principle. We are free from
the law, they say, bound only to keep it in spirit, if at all.

Implicit in this analysis, of course, is the thought that there is
a middle way between these two extremes and that this middle
way affords the truly Christian approach to living; but Paul
does not explicitly address this third alternative in the present
context. He merely deals with the extremes and leaves the middle ground to be largely only implicitly defined.

So Paul delineates and to an extent evaluates these two extremes: the one of *refusing* freedom, the failure to appreciate
and exercise our freedom in Christ, and the other the *abuse* of
freedom, as if freedom in Christ did away with all other elements of the gospel, including any authentic sense of living in
accordance with the standards of God. These two extremes will
direct our treatment of the law-versus-liberty theme.

Refusing Our Freedom (5:1-12)

Paul first takes up what must have been the central threat to the spiritual stability of the Galatians—the tendency to refuse to exercise and enjoy the freedom we have in Christ. They were tempted to compromise the gospel by accepting circumcision as a religious rite. This may have appeared to the Galatians to be a relatively innocent adherence to a cultural custom, but to Paul it was a serious compromise of the freedom of the gospel.

The modern reader, accustomed to thinking of circumcision in terms of a routine minor medical procedure, must not be misled into thinking that such a procedure is included in Paul's warning against compromising the gospel in this way. The routine medical practice of circumcising newly born male babies is modern, basically twentieth century and basically American. But it is not this medical use of circumcision that occupies Paul. He objects to the use of circumcision as a religious ritual thought of as necessary for incorporating the individual into the people of God.

Circumcision as a religious rite had a long and seemingly defensible history. After all, was it not commanded by God and almost equated with His covenant with Abraham (Genesis 17:10)? Yet even from its origins it should have been recognized as primarily symbolic of an inner attitude of the heart and mind. What God was most interested in was not the outward act of circumcision but the inward circumcision of the heart (Deuteronomy 10:16). This point Paul readily seized upon in another context, when he insisted that "a man is a Jew if he is one inwardly; and circumcision is circumcision of the heart" (Romans 2:29; see the whole paragraph beginning at verse 25).

We may look at Paul's remarks under three headings: accepting circumcision, rejecting circumcision and preaching circumcision.

Accepting Circumcision (Galatians 5:1-4)

Paul desires to impress upon the minds and hearts of his readers that accepting circumcision, as innocuous as it may appear, entails grave consequences that the recipient must carefully weigh.

First of all, one who accepts circumcision forfeits Christ. Paul's actual terms are that Christ would be of no value (5:2) and that such a person has been alienated from Christ (5:4). Such a one can also be said to have forfeited grace or to have fallen from grace (5:4), which amounts to much the same thing as forfeiting Christ.

In Paul's mind, this probably does not refer to the loss of salvation; other Pauline passages seem not to allow such a teaching and thus that kind of interpretation of these words would be inappropriate (see, for example, Romans 8:30).

Rather, he is referring to the fact that one who opts for an approach to salvation that relies on human activity or effort has cut himself off from the one God-provided means of receiving salvation, which is trust in the all-sufficiency of the Savior's provision. As long as we depend on works, we cannot be resting on the work of Christ; we cut ourselves off from it and therefore from any hope of righteousness before God.

Not only are Christ and His provisions forfeited by the one accepting circumcision, but also, in the second place, this kind of person takes upon himself the unbearable burden of keeping the whole of the law (Galatians 5:3). He is indebted to obey it all, clearly a debt that no human being can ever pay. Naturally, there is no way to win in this kind of approach.

That, maintains Paul, is the seriousness of accepting circumcision. One should therefore think carefully before committing oneself or others to such a move. In fact, it should be thoroughly and roundly rejected.

Rejecting Circumcision (5:5-10)

Instead of seeking refuge in the quick fix of a circumcision ritual performed once for all, we must commit ourselves to the slow, humanly difficult way of faith. We must walk the path of trust and hope, confident that we also have the help of the Spirit in sustaining us in what may be a long and arduous process of waiting.

On the other hand, we need to recognize that our trusting and waiting do not take place in an empty vacuum. Rather, this waiting is with the expectation of something real and glorious. Nevertheless, our full experience of righteousness is yet to come, and so at present it is only a hope of righteousness (5:5).

There is truth here that is implicitly relevant to the Christian's deeper life. In fact, there can be no deeper life at all apart from the attitude of trusting in the Lord. Relying on Him is the Christian's very breath. And often that trust will involve waiting, hoping, not seeing the fulfillment of our expectations (Hebrews 11:8; Romans 4:18-24). "We live by faith, not by sight" (2 Corinthians 5:7).

But there is also in this passage an indication that there exists for the Christian something beyond the deeper life, no matter what depth of walking with God we may have experienced—something that is not consummated in this life even in the most consecrated individual. The fullness of righteousness awaits us in the hereafter. And Paul never loses sight of this aspect of the Christian faith.

Still, if we are not to put our confidence in circumcision, neither are we to put it in the fact that we are uncircumcised (Galatians 5:6). That would be just as much a "work," and no work can justify us in the sight of God. The only thing that matters ultimately is our trust in the finished and perfect work of Christ on our behalf. That is all that counts as far as God is concerned.

But Paul never conceives of this saving faith apart from the fruit it produces in the form of works of love (5:6). The important thing to Paul is faith "expressing itself through love." Faith is never separated from obedience; rather we must obey the truth (5:7).

Ultimately, faith is being persuaded by, and hence trusting in, a God who has efficaciously called us to Himself (5:8). And for the Christian there can be nothing more trustworthy than the Almighty God who gives His word. If that kind of God has called us, how can we trust in anything else?

Furthermore, this warning against compromise is so radical that it insists on absolute rejection of all forms of erosion of the gospel message. All it takes is a little yeast to leaven the whole loaf (5:9). The least bit of compromise is deadly serious.

There is no way to salvation other than through trusting Christ. And there can be no addition whatsoever to this requirement of faith, as long as it is genuine trust in the sense defined above. Paul is confident that his hearers have understood and that they have accepted his line of argumentation (5:10).

Preaching Circumcision (5:10-12)

If Paul issues a stern warning to those who would embrace circumcision, his words for those who would urge others to accept it are even stronger: preaching circumcision is deserving of the judgment of God and is incompatible with preaching the cross—it is an extremely serious error.

First, there is a penalty to be paid by one who preaches circumcision. The text may not spell out exactly what this penalty will be, but it seems likely that Paul is simply restraining himself when speaking about ultimate divine judgment. And it does not matter who it is that preaches this false approach to salvation. There is no excuse one can make for compromising the gospel message.

On the other hand, Paul has a different situation in mind in First Corinthians when he talks about those who will be saved but only through fire (1 Corinthians 3:15). He is speaking of teachers who are basically preaching the correct message but the results of their efforts are not substantial; their works will not remain. In Galatians it is a matter of the teaching being so beyond the boundary of orthodoxy that it must be considered false teaching. For this kind of teacher there is reserved only severe judgment.

Secondly, preaching the erroneous doctrine of circumcision is incompatible with preaching the offense of the cross. One must choose. Paul could easily avoid persecution from the opponents by revising his theology into conformity with the circumcision party. This he refuses to do. He would rather suffer from the offense of the gospel that relies on the crucified Messiah than bask in the popularity of an easier, more inclusive gospel.

Paul concludes these remarks by noting the utter seriousness of leading others astray through proclamation of a false gospel. Rarely do we find such harsh and direct words as we find here in Galatians 5:12, where he wishes that the opponents "mutilate" or "emasculate" themselves. Paul's words also call into question the motives of the false teachers, who apparently by their insistence on the circumcision of the Galatian converts show little regard for the trouble they have caused them.

Although Paul has naturally cast his discussion of the failure to appreciate our freedom in Christ in the form of accepting or rejecting circumcision, we may certainly broaden our consideration of the application of his teaching. The question of circumcision does not for us have anything approaching the importance it had for the Galatians' situation. But there are other areas that throughout the history of the Church have, at least potentially, posed similar problems.

One of these is the ascetic tendency—the impulse to deny oneself the enjoyment of a particular activity even when the activity is not clearly forbidden by Scripture. Admittedly, there may be a legitimate ascetic strain in authentic Christian faith, and undoubtedly some of the great Christian ascetics would not have been castigated by Paul the way he has dealt with the Galatians and those who were insisting on their circumcision. Nevertheless, it is certainly conceivable that asceticism could be taken to the extreme of maintaining its necessity for a good Christian life or even for salvation. If that were the case, it would surely have been opposed by Paul in the same emphatic terms he used to denounce his opponents in Galatia.

The apostle's discussion of the weaker brother is also germane. It is clear that the weaker brother is a Christian, but a Christian who has scruples in the area of Christian liberty that other Christians—perhaps the majority of Christians—do not have. It is also clear that Paul sides with the correct understanding of the broader ethical perspective. The items that are questionable or wrong to the weaker Christian are not in themselves wrong for Paul. He, of course, is willing to set aside his Christian liberty, lest he cause one of the weaker believers to stumble. But in principle he is committed to the less ascetic outlook that views the activities in question as legitimate for the believer whose conscience does not forbid participation (1 Corinthians 8, 10; Romans 14).

Even though this discussion of the weaker conscience is distantly relevant to Paul's treatment of circumcision, it is still quite different. The weaker Christian is still a Christian, whereas the Judaizer has cut himself off from Christ. True, the weak person may violate his conscience, engage in something that his conscience tells him not to do and thereby incur spiritual damage. But it is not the weakness itself that is condemned—only its compromise. On the other hand, it is the Judaizers' fundamental position of insisting on circumcision that is at fault.

Abusing Our Freedom (Galatians 5:13-15)

Now Paul acknowledges that Christian freedom can be bent in the opposite direction to justify harmful behavior. In this perspective our liberty in Christ is seen as freeing us from the restraints even of the moral law. But, he says, this way of interpreting freedom in Christ ought not to be.

This libertarian abuse of freedom is wrong first of all because it is self-indulgent. It allows the sinful nature, the flesh, to have its way and thus can be harmful in all sorts of ways, not least to oneself.

This misuse of freedom is also self-destructive in another way, as 5:15 clearly shows. The more we bend our freedom, the more our actions may come back to haunt us. If we, through neglect of the moral law and especially the law of neighbor-love, devour a fellow-believer, we ourselves run the great risk of being destroyed by others because of our actions.

But the antidote to this antinomian abuse of freedom is to recognize that Christian freedom is not so much freedom *outside* of law as it is freedom *within* law interpreted as an expression of the standards and will of God. It is a freedom that must line up with the commandment regarding neighbor-love. And since that command summarizes the entire law, the believer may gain insight and direction from other aspects of the moral law of God. In this sense God's law guides and informs our Christian freedom to keep us from its antinomian misuse. The believer is never freed from the law of love to neighbor. Rather, we are to serve one another in love.

There is no better biblical example of the misuse of freedom than the action of the prodigal son during the time of his riotous living. Though the details are not supplied beyond the description that this phase of his life was "wild," it does not take much in the way of imagination to fill out the substance of what that kind of living must have involved. He later described it as sinning against God as well as sinning against the principles his father had inculcated in him. Clearly it was a style of living that had thrown off all traces of conforming to moral values. It was libertine and licentious and stands as a memorable and permanently delineated type of what this lifestyle entails. But in effect, it is no freedom at all, but a bondage to the basest elements of human nature.

Of course, this example is not a pure example of the misuse of specifically *Christian* freedom. It does, however, offer a particularly noteworthy presentation of the libertine tendency that may exist in both Christian and non-Christian alike.

Moreover, the kind of licentious attitude represented by the prodigal son finds many echoes in the experiences of subsequent generations. We turn once again to Augustine for an especially vivid example. In a passage that does not so much dwell on the precise nature of his libertarian life, he too gives expression to the fact that what seems to be freedom is really an unwitting bondage. Listen to the account of his trying to influence a friend in a libertine direction:

> For my part I answered his arguments by pointing to the example of married men who had been lovers of wisdom, had served God well, and had retained the affection of their friends, whom they had loyally loved in return. But I was far from being the equal of these noble spirits. I was bowed down by this disease of the flesh. Its deadly pleasures were a chain that I dragged along with me, yet I was afraid to be freed from it; and I refused to accept the good advice of Alypius, repelling the hand that meant to loose my bonds.[1]

Thus Augustine came to recognize that the apparent freedom of libertine living concealed beneath its surface an actual bondage.

We owe to Mark Twain an interesting story that likewise helps us visualize the deceptiveness of apparent freedom. His book is entitled *Pudd'nhead Wilson*, and it relates a tale about two look-alike baby boys of the old South. The white boy, Tom, was the son of the master, while Chambers, being only ninety-seven percent white, would have been relegated to a life of slavery, except that his mother Roxy one day switched the boys, thinking to have her son raised free. And to a certain extent he would have outwardly enjoyed a life of freedom. Thus Tom was raised as Chambers and Chambers as Tom. However, the hoped-for freedom for Roxy's son turned out to be in name only. He fell into a life of dissolution from which he could never bring himself to escape. His liberty was in a real sense illusory.

It is certainly possible to turn the appearance/reality dynamic around, so that one who is physically subjugated in one way or another can in reality be free. Paul and Silas, for example, may have been physically incarcerated at Philippi, but their spirits were obviously at liberty in the Lord, singing His praises in spite of their dire surroundings (Acts 16:23-25).

Conclusion

Paul has probed the two extremes of neglecting freedom and abusing freedom. He has left the middle ground largely uncharted in his discussion, or at least its general contours are only implicitly sketched. But there surely is an implied middle way in the use of Christian liberty, and that is to view it as liberty within the context of law. As Paul says elsewhere, "I am not free from God's law but am under Christ's law" (1 Corinthians 9:21).

The balance between liberty and law is nowhere better illustrated than in the account of the decision the first church council at Jerusalem arrived at regarding the obligations of Gentile believers. On the one hand, it was emphatically concluded that the newly won Gentile Christians would not be required to be circumcised or keep the entire law of Moses (Acts 15:5, 19). But on the other hand, this freedom did not permit the Gentiles to engage in any conduct they saw fit. Even practices that would not necessarily be wrong for Gentiles but would be offensive to Jews and Jewish Christians in their respective localities they were encouraged to forgo out of courtesy toward these others. Such voluntary restrictions are not really to be considered the loss of freedom.

It is in this balance between liberty and law that we experience the maturity of Christian living, a maturity that is of the essence of the deeper life. Deeper Christian living implies abandonment to God. And that can scarcely be thought of apart from taking upon oneself the yoke of His authority, the expression of which is His moral law.

There is a bondage to the Divine Master that is at the same time a freedom in the truest sense of the word. In His service there is perfect freedom, as the collect in the Book of Common Prayer so eloquently puts it. That is the kind of liberty we have in Christ. Let us enjoy it to the full.

> My glorious Victor, Prince divine,
>   clasp these surrendered hands in Thine;
> At length my will is all Thine own,
>   glad vassal of a Saviour's throne.
> My Master, lead me to Thy door;
>   pierce this now willing ear once more;
> Thy bonds are freedom; let me stay
>   with Thee to toil, endure, obey.
> Yes, ear and hand, and thought, and will—

> use all in Thy dear slavery still!
> Self's weary liberties I cast
>   beneath Thy feet; there keep them fast.
> Tread them still down; and then, I know,
>   these hands shall with Thy gifts o'erflow;
> And pierced ears shall hear the tone
>   which tells me Thou and I are one.[2]

Questions for Reflection or Discussion

1. What does Paul mean by "fallen away from grace" (Galatians 5:4)?

2. What does it mean to await righteousness and hope for it (5:5)?

3. What is implied in the words, "You were running a good race" (5:7)?

4. What is implied in the words, "I am confident in the Lord" (5:10)?

5. What is the penalty that will be paid by the one throwing the Galatians into confusion (5:10)?

6. What obligations do we have to "one another" (5:13-15)?

7. What does "the entire law is summed up in a single command" mean (5:14)?

Endnotes

1. Augustine, *Confessions*, Book VI, chapter 12; trans. R.S. Pine-Coffin.
2. Handley C.G. Moule, "My Glorious Victor," *Hymns of the Christian Life* (Camp Hill, PA: Christian Publications, 1978), # 263.

11

The Spirituality of Paul's Gospel

Galatians 5:16-26

So I say, live by the Spirit, and you will not gratify the desires of the sinful nature. For the sinful nature desires what is contrary to the Spirit, and the Spirit what is contrary to the sinful nature. They are in conflict with each other, so that you do not do what you want. But if you are led by the Spirit, you are not under law.

The acts of the sinful nature are obvious: sexual immorality, impurity and debauchery; idolatry and witchcraft; hatred, discord, jealousy, fits of rage, selfish ambition, dissensions, factions and envy; drunkenness, orgies, and the like. I warn you, as I did before, that those who live like this will not inherit the kingdom of God.

But the fruit of the Spirit is love, joy, peace, patience, kindness, goodness, faithfulness, gentleness and self-control. Against such things there is no law. Those who belong to Christ Jesus have crucified the sinful nature with its passions and desires. Since we live by the Spirit, let us keep in step with the Spirit. Let us not become conceited, provoking and envying each other.

The full course of the argumentation is over. There remains for Paul the task of applying his gospel in practical ways for the enabling of the Galatians to foster spirituality in their Christian lives.

In our day it is becoming increasingly popular to speak of Christian living as a kind of spirituality, although just exactly what is meant by this term may differ from author to author. One scholar may emphasize spirituality as meditation, another define it as engaging in liturgical ritual, another as attempting to improve the social circumstances of the needy, and still others seeing spirituality as fulfilled in a life of personal morality. There certainly is no fully agreed upon view of what spirituality is. Thus we may legitimately invoke individuals of widely differing perspectives as examples of spirituality.

For example, the spirituality of Mother Theresa consisted in her loving care for those in physical need. On the other hand, we might see Billy Graham's spirituality to consist, at least in part, in his uncompromising fidelity to the gospel message and his integrity in his dealings with financial affairs and people in authority. Yet another example of "spirituality" is A.B. Simpson's compassionate heart for the spiritual needs of the lost. And there may be still other ways of identifying and illustrating what may legitimately be called authentic spirituality.

But however that may be, for Paul spirituality clearly means walking according to the Spirit. Thus Paul approaches spirituality in this section as something that consists of and issues in behavior that is broadly speaking in the realm of the ethical and moral. At the same time, it seeks to avoid those actions that fall short of God's standards.

Paul's application of the gospel to Christian spirituality begins with a section depicting a conflict in which the believer is involved (5:16-18).

This conflict is not the struggle with forces external to the believer, as Paul discusses in Ephesians 6; that is, it is not in this present context the struggle "against the rulers, against the authorities, against the powers of this dark world and against the spiritual forces of evil in the heavenly realms," as we find in the Ephesians passage (6:12). Rather, it is a tension within the believer's own personal experience—an opposition between "flesh" and Spirit.

The result of this conflict of flesh and Spirit, as long as it remains unresolved, is that the believer experiences a tension between the will to do what is right and the fulfillment of what is desired. "You do not do what you want," he says (Galatians 5:17). Yet even in this introductory statement of the issue, Paul alludes to the believer's dynamic in the struggle—the help of the Spirit's leading.[1]

Moreover, this reference to the Spirit is indeed a reference to the Spirit's *help*. Paul's sense is that if the believer walks or lives by the Spirit, he or she will not gratify the desires of the sinful nature. Unfortunately, the matter is somewhat clouded by the mistranslation "do not gratify" found in the Revised Standard Version. Rather, it should be translated "you *will* not gratify," indicating a promise rather than a command. The promise concerns what will happen in the believer's life, and the statement about walking in the Spirit is the condition under which that promise will be fulfilled.[2] Paraphrased, the verse means that if we live by the Spirit, we will not gratify the desires of the sinful nature.

After this introductory section, Paul develops his theme by showing the two alternative approaches to living and then gives the reasons why the Christian should opt for the one and not the other.

The Way of the Flesh (5:19-21)

This list of vices is not meant to be exhaustive. This is first of all indicated by the phrase "and the like." Thus there are other items similar to these which could have been added to the list. Some important vices, such as lying or pride, are not present at all, but would clearly fit under the category of things proscribed.

Furthermore, there appears to be some overlapping of terms since some of them are difficult to distinguish (dissensions, factions). So it seems wise to understand Paul's list of items to be merely illustrative of the kinds of behavior that are the antithesis to sound Christian living.

There is considerable discussion about whether or not the list is intended to be arranged in any logical order. While some doubt may remain, the treatment by the NIV as indicated by the punctuation is as good as any, in which four overall categories are seen. First, there are three sexual sins (sexual immorality, impurity, debauchery). These are then followed by two vices diametrically opposed to all that the gospel stands for (idolatry, witchcraft). Then come eight vices of attitude and spirit (hatred, discord, jealousy, fits of rage, selfish ambition, dissensions, factions, envy). The concluding two have to do with excess in the sphere of drunkenness (drunkenness, orgies).

What is quite noteworthy in the list, especially in view of the fact that the items are called works of the flesh (the NIV paraphrases "works of the flesh" as "acts of the sinful nature"), is the prominence given to those vices that are not particularly fleshly as that term is commonly understood. Over half of the sins listed here have more to do with the mind and the will than with the flesh in any physical sense. And yet these too are called acts of the flesh. It is no doubt for this reason that several translations have paraphrased the term "flesh" as referring more broadly to human sinful nature in general. These are the deeds that flow naturally from any perspective that is hostile to God or any attempt to construct moral living in purely human terms.

The Christian is to have nothing to do with any of these or similar qualities. In fact, Paul is insistent that to engage in them is to forfeit God's kingdom. Paul does not mean, of course, that one momentary lapse into one of these vices renders the person committing the act liable to eternal damnation. Rather, it is someone who persistently lives the kind of life characterized by such acts that is in danger of God's eternal judgment.

Moreover, this is a teaching he had consistently proclaimed from the beginning of his contacts with the Galatians. Apparently, it was never too early, in Paul's mind, to confront believers, or even inquirers, with the moral and ethical claims of the gospel and to warn people about God's judgment on human depravity.

Way of the Spirit (5:22-23)

But there is another way—the way of the Spirit. Let us consider first some general principles pertaining to the way of the Spirit and then look at some of the specific aspects of the Spirit's fruit in the believer's life.

In general

Like the former catalog of vices, this list of virtues is also representative rather than complete, as is indicated by the word "such," when we read "against such things there is no law" (5:23). Moreover, once again certain of the terms appear to be somewhat overlapping. It is not immediately obvious, for example, how terms like kindness and goodness should be distinguished. So we should understand the list to be illustrative of the manifold gifts and graces that are wrought in and through the Christian by the ministry of the Holy Spirit.

But in this list it is much more difficult than it is in the previous one to detect an intended order of arrangement. Of course, the first term, love, can easily be taken, in a sense, as embracing many of the others. In this regard it is useful to compare this current list of virtues with Paul's description of love in First Corinthians 13, where a number of items in the present list, such as patience and kindness, are there subsumed under the category of love.

Beyond this, however, it is largely speculation as to any arrangement. Yet it is at least interesting that of the last eight terms, the two that are at the center of these are the two nearly identical qualities of kindness and goodness. Furthermore, the terms next to the center—patience and faithfulness—have a common stress on steadfastness; and peace and gentleness, the next pair, likewise have a certain commonality to them. It might be thought that this way of seeing correspondence between the various items could be carried through consistently. But then the otherwise tempting appearance of a chiastic structure is marred by an inability to match joy and self-control in any meaningful way.[3] So any detection of order in the list must remain tentative.

What are we to make of the singular "fruit"? We need to remember that the word is another of those words that have not only singular and plural forms, but also have a collective sense. Thus the use of a collective term does not necessarily rule out a plural understanding. At the same time, there may be merit to the suggestion that by using the collective sense Paul intends all of these qualities to exist, to some extent at least, in every believer, not distributed among the body of believers as are the spiritual gifts mentioned in other passages (see especially 1 Corinthians 12:8-10, 28-30; Romans 12:6-8).

A further general introductory point is the question whether any of these virtues attributed to the work of the Holy Spirit are similar to virtues going by the same names or other names in the common Greco-Roman culture of the day. Presumably most of these terms denoted something to the ordinary reader of Greek. And the fact that they are here said to be the work of the Spirit does not preclude the possibility that they could also be understood as common virtues of the day. If they, or at least some of them, are seen as common virtues, the Spirit's role would be to enhance qualities already present rather than to create qualities *de novo*.

This is not to say that all Spirit-produced virtues are simply enhancements of common virtues. Nor does it imply that there might not be counterfeit qualities in the secular realm masquerading as those in the spiritual.

It should not be overlooked that the qualities enumerated here as appropriate for the believer and wrought in the believer's life by the Spirit are the very qualities that are manifest both in God the Father and God the Son. In this way, the believer is called to an imitation of Christ and of the Father.

Finally, Paul's concluding statement in Galatians 5:23, "Against such things there is no law" seems to have much the same meaning as his earlier statement in 5:18, "But if you are led by the Spirit, you are not under law." That is, for anyone who truly exhibits the characteristics embodied in the list of virtues, there is nothing that the law can add or needs to address. The person is complete without the influence of the law.

In particular

From these general remarks concerning the fruit of the Spirit we now turn to consider specific aspects of that fruit. While it may not be profitable to discuss all these virtues extensively, it would be appropriate to review some of the more important and distinctive of them.

First of all, the love Paul has in mind as the product of the Spirit is surely to be understood as a love that exists on a high plane. It goes without saying that this is a self-giving love. It is not self-seeking (1 Corinthians 13:5), but seeks the good of others.

It would be wrong, however, to try, as is commonly done, to connect this idea of self-giving love exclusively with the group of Greek words represented by the word *agape*. This can be demonstrated in a number of ways.

First, the other main Greek word-group expressing love (*phil-*) can also be used to convey the idea of self-giving love, or at least a love of the highest possible quality. For occasionally God the Father is said to love His Son with this kind of love (for example, John 5:20).

And furthermore, there are a few instances when an *agape*-type word speaks of something considerably less than self-giving love. For example, Jesus says that even the tax collectors love (*agap-*) those who love them (Matthew 5:46). Certainly this speaks of a reciprocal love, not one that is essentially self-giving.[4]

So it appears futile to link the idea of self-giving love with a particular Greek word or group of words. Nevertheless, although it may not be possible to associate it exclusively with a single form of expression, still we cannot doubt that there is such a thing as self-giving love, and it is that about which Paul is writing in the present context.

There can be no more perfect illustration of self-giving love than that provided by the Lord Jesus Himself. "Greater love has no one than this, that he lay down his life for his friends" (John 15:13). In fact, so self-giving is this love of Christ for us that it caused Him to die for us while we were yet in our state of ungodliness and sin (Romans 5:6-8).

There may be an occasional example of self-giving love in the world, but much of the time the love that exists in the world is but a pale reflection of the self-giving love Paul claims is a product of the Spirit's presence in the life of the true believer.

In a similar fashion, the joy that is produced by the Spirit is distinct in concept from any joy that may be a part of our common human experience. In this sense, joy is first of all a delight in the Lord Himself. Secondly, it is delight in the gifts of God, and since these gifts are all around us as a result of God's common grace, there is very much for which to be joyful. Thus we can find joy in a beautiful work of art. But it is not joy to the fullest unless and until it finds its ultimate delight in the God who is the source of the gift. Whether we call such a high level of delight "joy" or "happiness" is not really the issue. What distinguishes the highest level of Christian joy from any lower level of enjoyment is simply that Christian joy delights ultimately in the Lord.

Likewise in the area of peace, the Scripture distinguishes between the peace that Christ can give from that which is found through other sources. As He says, "Peace I leave with you; my peace I give you. I do not give to you as the world gives" (John 14:27).

Christ's peace is, of course, a peace that can exist in the presence of difficulty. Again He says, "I have told you these things, so that in me you may have peace. In this world you will have trouble. But take heart! I have overcome the world" (16:33). So the peace of Christ can exist in the midst of trouble. And the next item, patience, is closely related, being the attitude that can trustingly accept the trouble and bear up under it.

Probably Paul is here referring to any and all aspects of peace that the Christian may have. This would include not only peace with God resulting from forgiveness of sins (Romans 5:1), or an inner peace that is able to accept the difficulties encountered in faithfully following the Lord, but also the peace that can and should exist between members of the family of faith (Ephesians 4:3). All of these are the product of the Spirit.

As to kindness and goodness, it is probably not very helpful to be too specific about their nature. What we can say is that they are also qualities in which the Christian is not only aided by the Spirit, but ones in which the Christian is distinctly imitating the same attributes in God. As Jesus said, we are to do *good,* and if we do, we will be sons of the Most High, because He is *kind* (Luke 6:35).

The next term is the one normally throughout the New Testament translated "faith" but probably here correctly translated "faithfulness." However, the fact that a word may legitimately have two different meanings should not lead us to think that the two meanings are really one and the same, or that an author has both meanings in mind when the word is used. It is a very common occurrence in language that a word may have more than one meaning and, for that matter, that two words may have the same meaning.

The reason for opting for faithfulness in this context rather than faith (as in the KJV) is that such an interpretation of the word as indicating an ethical quality seems to be more appropriate in view of the fact that the other terms in the list designate similar qualities.

Faithfulness combines the idea of being trustworthy with that of steadfastness. A faithful person can be trusted and depended on, especially over a period of time. It is perhaps best described in Christ's parable of the talents, in which the master says to two of his servants, "Well done, good and faithful servant! You have been faithful with a few things; I will put you in charge of many things" (Matthew 25:21, 23). The reward for such faithfulness is enjoyment of the Lord's presence (Revelation 2:10).

But like many of the terms in Paul's list, this one also may mean not only fidelity to God but also fidelity to His people. Such appears to be Paul's thought, for example, in Colossians 1:7, where he describes Epaphras as "a faithful minister of Christ on our behalf," implying that he faithfully served Christ by faithfully serving Paul. And even when the term is not present in the text, it is not difficult to see beautiful examples of faithful service, as when certain women helped support Jesus and His disciples as they traveled throughout Galilee (Luke 8:1-3).

The last two characteristics—gentleness and self-control—have a good deal in common. Self-control is the ability to curb excesses in one's character, whether these be excesses in sexual appetite, excesses in alcoholic drinking,[5] outbursts of anger or any one of a number of other ways people find it difficult to control themselves. If one is able by the Spirit so to control the personality, one will thereby exhibit the quality of gentleness.

But self-control and gentleness do not necessarily rule out the kind of "righteous indignation" displayed at times by Christ. We naturally recall his indignation at the money changers (John 2:14-17), as well as His anger before the tomb of Lazarus (11:33, 38).[6]

On the other hand, we can also recall instances of Christ's truly remarkable self-control, as in the almost complete silence at His trial, not even defending Himself against the unjust and untrue accusations that were being hurled at Him (Mark 14:61).[7]

Way of the Christian (5:24-26)

So there are two ways—the way of the flesh and the way of the Spirit. And there is no question as to which direction the Christian should go, which one of the two ways the believer should follow. One who belongs to Christ must walk with the Spirit.

The first step toward victory in the Christian's struggle with the flesh is the recognition—we might even say "reckoning"—that a decisive break with the sinful nature took place at the moment of conversion. At that time, in the believer's identification with Christ in His death and resurrection, there was, says Paul, a crucifixion of the flesh. The struggle may go on, but the believer ought never to forget the fact that implied in the act of coming to Christ for salvation is an act of repentance, of turning one's back on sin and the sinful nature.

Further, if it is true that we have crucified our sinful nature at the time of our conversion, it is no less true that we have been brought to life by the Spirit: we live by the Spirit. This truth likewise undergirds our life as Christians. The old nature has been dealt a decisive blow, and we have been made alive by the Spirit of God. Let us then conduct our lives accordingly.

The other aspect of experiencing spiritual victory is "keeping in step with" the Spirit. Paul, of course, is not giving any easy, foolproof formula for attaining spirituality or Christian maturity, but he is offering the way of holiness that is unique to his gospel and to Christianity in general. That is the help of God. As difficult as it may be to walk by the Spirit, at least the believer is not left alone, but has the Spirit of God to walk beside him and even in front, leading the way.

Conclusion

The fruit of the Spirit is presented to us first as an assurance that God is truly at work in His own. If we belong to Christ, we have His Spirit dwelling within us. And if the Spirit is dwelling within us, He will produce His fruit in us to some extent at least.

But it is difficult not to see it also as a standard toward which we must strive. These graces produced by the Spirit represent at the same time the kind of people we ought to be. Thus the fruit of the Spirit is both promise and obligation, both comfort and command, both our confidence and a call to holiness.

It would be impossible to illustrate with justice each one of these aspects of the fruit of Spirit, but perhaps the primary one—love—could be further developed. We have seen that what the Spirit expects and imparts is self-giving love. But we must realize that this self-giving love may take an amazing variety of forms.

On some occasions self-giving love may involve the literal giving of one's life for the sake of others. High in the mountains of Japan is a place known as Shiokari Pass, accessible only by a steep mountain railway. Its difficulty of access may present a potentially dangerous situation even under the most ideal circumstances. But if a train ever got out of control, it would surely accelerate so as to result in great tragedy and loss of life. On just such a train was a young Christian man, whose devotion to the service of Christ was remarkable, given the thoroughly anti-Christian climate in which he had been raised. He had prepared himself well for a long life of serving his Lord. But when moment of need came, he knew what he had to do, and threw himself out in front of the train to stop it, saving the lives of the others on board from almost certain destruction.[8] That is self-giving love.

A very different form of self-giving love is that shown by Benjamin B. Warfield, the renowned theologian and New Testament scholar. Although being extremely productive academically and able to pursue an amazing amount of valuable research and writing, for years he lovingly and tenderly cared for his invalid wife. No task undertaken for her care was too menial for him, in view of the self-giving love residing in his heart through the Spirit.

Readers of the books of John Grisham will remember the self-sacrificing love of his unforgettable character Rachel Lane, who had given up just about everything to serve God as a missionary in a remote jungle area in South America. Such was her love for Christ and for her people that she immersed herself in this primitive work, having very little contact with the outside world. Not only had she voluntarily committed herself to serving in these difficult conditions, but also she had denied herself the joys of marriage and family life and, as unbelievable as it may seem, had turned her back on a bequest worth 11 *bil-*

lion dollars just to pour out her life in service to a tribe who had never heard the good news about Christ.[9]

We might recall also the story of the Ten Boom family of *The Hiding Place* fame. Theirs was a self-giving love that not only shielded innocent folk from extreme danger, but also was willing to undergo the great personal hardship of incarceration in order to protect them.

But perhaps the most amazing example of self-giving love, other than that of the Lord Himself, is the case of the Apostle Paul, when he said, "For I could wish that I myself were cursed and cut off from Christ for the sake of my brothers, those of my own race, the people of Israel" (Romans 9:3-4). He was willing not only to die, but to die eternally. It was a wish that was never fulfilled, nor could it have been fulfilled; nevertheless, it stands as a graphic portrayal of what might be called the ultimate in self-giving love.

So love may take many forms, and it may not be that we will ever be asked to give of ourselves in any of these ways. But are we willing to show self-giving love in the way the Lord calls us to, whatever that may be?

Such issues get to the very heart of the deeper life. The deeper life is a life of the Spirit. It is this Spirit that is the source and substance of the Christian's spirituality. Let us not seek for some other form of spirituality. All the spirituality we will ever need is found in the Holy Spirit of God and especially in the fruit and graces He produces in the life of the believer.

> I want a principle within of jealous, godly fear,
> A sensibility of sin, a pain to feel it near.
>> I want the first approach to feel of pride or fond
>>> desire,
>> To catch the wandering of my will, and quench the
>>> kindling fire.
> That I from Thee no more may part, no more Thy

goodness grieve,
The filial awe, the supple heart, the tender conscience
give.
Quick as the apple of the eye, O God, my
conscience make.
Awake my soul when sin is nigh, and keep it still
awake.
O may the least omission pain my well instructed soul,
And drive me to the blood again, which makes the
wounded whole.[10]

Questions for Reflection or Discussion

1. Is "you will not gratify" a prediction or a command (Galatians 5:16)?
2. How is it possible to "not do what you want" (5:17)?
3. In what sense are we not under law (5:18)?
4. What does it mean to "*live*" like this" (5:21)?
5. What does it mean to *inherit* the kingdom of God (5:21)?
6. What is the relationship between the crucifixion mentioned in 5:24 and that in 2:20?

Endnotes

1. The word "if" in 5:18 is not as hypothetical as it may sound. It makes an assumption but does not necessarily doubt the truth of the assumption. And there is no reason to doubt its truth here.
2. Frederick F. Bruce, *The Epistle to the Galatians: A Commentary on the Greek Text* (Grand Rapids: Eerdmans, 1982), 243.
3. An alternative arrangement would divide the list into three groups of three virtues each.
4. The same point made here about Greek words can also be made about the Hebrew word for love, *ahav*. It may speak of self-giving love, as in the commandment to love one's neighbor (Leviticus 19:18). But it may

also be used to designate the lowest forms of lust, as in Amnon's feelings toward Tamar (2 Samuel 13:15).

5. Compare the concluding items in the list of vices—drunkenness, orgies.

6. The NIV has toned this down to a statement about Jesus being deeply moved, but it should probably be taken as a much stronger emotional response. See Donald A. Carson, *The Gospel According to John* (Grand Rapids: Eerdmans, 1991), 415-417.

7. In this way He fulfilled the prophecy in Isaiah 53:7.

8. Ayako Miura, *Shiokari Pass* (Old Tappan, NJ: Fleming H. Revell, 1974).

9. John Grisham, *The Testament* (New York: Doubleday, 1999).

10. Charles Wesley, "I Want a Principle Within" (a hymn).

12

The Ministry
of Paul's Gospel

Galatians 6:1-10

Brothers, if someone is caught in a sin, you who are spiritual should restore him gently. But watch yourself, or you also may be tempted. Carry each other's burdens, and in this way you will fulfill the law of Christ. If anyone thinks he is something when he is nothing, he deceives himself. Each one should test his own actions. Then he can take pride in himself, without comparing himself to somebody else, for each one should carry his own load.

Anyone who receives instruction in the word must share all good things with his instructor.

Do not be deceived: God cannot be mocked. A man reaps what he sows. The one who sows to please his sinful nature, from that nature will reap destruction; the one who sows to please the Spirit, from the Spirit will reap eternal life. Let us not become weary in doing good, for at the proper time we will reap a harvest if we do not give up. Therefore, as we have opportunity, let us do good to all people, especially to those who belong to the family of believers.

From the general discussion of Christian living outlined in the previous section, Paul now turns to its more specific outworking, primarily focusing on how the believer can and should minister to others. The material seems to break down naturally into the following sections: ministry to other believers, to oneself, to Christian leaders and to all people.

Ministry to Other Believers (6:1-2)

While he does not explicitly say so, it is probable that Paul has in mind in this paragraph the ministering to believers— both, first of all, a specific ministry of restoration and then a more general ministry of support.

Ministry of restoration (6:1)

The ministry of restoration is a ministry by the spiritual Christian to the sinning believer. But by the "spiritual" Paul does not mean a special class of Christians set apart either by the particularly high degree of holiness they have attained or by their elected or appointed position in the church. In one sense, all believers, as we have seen, are "spiritual"; they are people of the Spirit, born of the Spirit, indwelt by the Spirit, guided by the Spirit, empowered by the Spirit. But when a believer falls into sin, he or she needs the help of those in whom the Spirit's work has not been so completely disrupted by the abnormality of sin.

Our Lord's own instruction not to seek to cast a speck out of our brother's eye while we have a plank in our own eye is germane here (Matthew 7:3-5). On the one hand, like the present passage, it exercises caution and humility. On the other hand, that passage may sometimes be mistakenly assumed to mean that we should never call attention to sin in our brother's life. But if that were the case, there could be no ministry of restoration possible, or at least it would be restricted to cases where the sinning brother or sister has initiated the process. Actually, Christ's words simply caution against its misuse. For He very carefully and deliberately says, "*First* take the plank out of your own eye, and *then* you will see clearly to remove the speck from your brother's eye." Thus it is not absolutely forbidden to point out another's fault in hope of correcting unspiritual behavior and bringing the person back into fellowship with the Lord and with the believing community. In fact, such care for a fellow believer may actually be encouraged.

A particularly colorful example in Scripture of a rather bold instance of restoring a sinful brother is the way Nathan confronted David with his double sin of adultery with Bathsheba and the subsequent murder of her husband Uriah, not to mention his attempts to cover up both of these transgressions. If at first Nathan was indirect and polite as he recounted his parable of a rich man who had unscrupulously oppressed a poor man, he was both bold and direct in his classic, accusatory words to David, "Thou art the man" (2 Samuel 12:7, KJV). And in that particular case, such boldness was indeed used by God to bring about the desired repentance and restoration, so that the Lord could actually take away David's sin (12:13). Boldness may sometimes, perhaps rarely, but sometimes be called for as a means of restoration.

On the other hand, sin's potential to disrupt the Christian life is present for all believers, so that most ministry of restoration must be carried out with a great deal of gentleness and humbleness. So Paul adds the admonition to examine oneself, just as Jesus urged us to look at our own eye before we look at another's. There can be no blindness to one's own sinfulness. And the great temptation is to take pride in one's spirituality that enables one to engage in a ministry of restoration. Paul implicitly cautions us about both of these potentially present dangers—hypocrisy and pride.

In this regard the treatment of the adulterous woman by Christ is a model for us to follow (John 8:3-11). He did not condemn her in the way that her accusers manifestly thought appropriate by demanding her punishment. On the other hand, neither did He condone her sinful act. It was a gracious and gentle effort toward restoration that the Lord administered; and, as far as we know, the desired result was achieved.[1]

The challenge to us in all of this is to make sure that we are in such a condition of spirituality that we may be used of the Lord to minister to an erring fellow believer. Once again we are called to true spirituality, to the deeper life principle of being in tune with the Spirit and sensitive to His leading. Only in this way can we hope to fulfill Paul's exhortation that is before us.

Ministry of support (Galatians 6:2)

"Carry each other's burdens." This injunction is not to be thought of as merely a restatement of the previous verse, as if bearing another's burden is simply another way of speaking about restoring a brother. For it is the spiritual who are to restore, whereas the burden bearing is here spoken of as a mutual responsibility.

On the other hand, though it is not a mere restatement, it may be taken as a broader, more inclusive statement, including the kinds of problems expressly in view in 6:1, but also including ministry that is not specifically restorative either in its design or in its effect. If we do see the verse in this way, we may understand the "spiritual" to have a special responsibility to offer the kind of support that all Christians have some obligation to demonstrate toward one another.

That the burdens experienced are broader than those contemplated in 6:1 is supported by the concept of mutual support as it is more generally stated in First Corinthians: "If one part suffers, every part suffers with it" (12:26). Furthermore, in another passage Paul seems to imply that any of the difficulties that arise from our existence in this body may be considered burdens. "For while we are in this tent, we groan and are burdened" (2 Corinthians 5:4).[2] So the burdens that we are to bear for one another are not limited to burdens of the guilt and shame resulting from transgression of God's law. We are to help each other bear them, whatever kind of burden they are.

Even this more general obligation to support one another is, to be sure, but an extension of the law requiring the love of one's neighbor. In this context, however, it is called the law of Christ. But this phrase does not imply, of course, that it is anything different from the same command to love the neighbor as it is found in the Old Testament law.[3]

Ministry to Self (Galatians 6:3-5)

In all the consideration of what it means to minister to others, Paul does not neglect to ponder the proper and improper ways in which we need to attend to ourselves, that we not become either conceited and proud, or so self-abasing that we, in effect, dishonor the Creator and His handiwork in us.

While it is clearly wrong to overestimate one's status ("if anyone thinks he is something when he is nothing" [6:3]), it is apparently not sinful for a person to have a realistic appraisal of how he is doing in fulfilling the obligation God has particularly laid on him. A similar balance between right and wrong self-appraisal is struck by Paul in Romans 12:3: "Do not think of yourself more highly than you ought, but rather think of yourself with sober judgment." That is not false depreciation, but realistic self-appraisal.

The apostle is himself a superb example of what it means to maintain the balance between proper humility and the recognition of one's God-bestowed gifts and abilities.

On the one hand, we think of his statement about being the least of all the apostles, not even deserving to be called an

apostle, because he had persecuted the Church of God (1 Corinthians 15:9). He can even refer to himself as "less than the
least of all God's people" (Ephesians 3:8) and the chief of
sinners (1 Timothy 1:15, KJV).

On the other hand, when it came to assessing realistically the
way God had equipped him for ministry, a number of passages
come to mind. Even in the passages just cited, in which Paul expressed such deep humility, he could add: "But by the grace of
God I am what I am" (1 Corinthians 15:10) and "This grace was
given me: to preach to the Gentiles the unsearchable riches of
Christ" (Ephesians 3:8). He can refer to his "insight into the
mystery of Christ" (3:4), and, as we have seen, call the gospel
of Christ "my gospel."[4] Moreover, he can even "boast" about
his ministry and authority in the Lord (2 Corinthians
10:1–12:6; note especially 10:8, 13; 11:22-29). So Paul's sense
of self-worth in the Lord is far from a self-deprecating false humility.

What can go wrong in any attempt to evaluate oneself is to
compare our level of conformity to God's expectations with the
level that others may have attained or be expected to attain. In
one sense, God has applied His standard of behavior for us to
all of us in much the same way. Thus, we are all expected to
manifest at least some of the fruit of the Spirit, as we have already seen. In fact, without such a display of the Spirit's fruit in
our lives, we could wonder whether we are actually people of
the Spirit at all.

Nevertheless, there appears to be here an individualization in
the bearing of the burden of fulfilling God's standard. We
should not overlook the little word "for" that connects the two
statements in Galatians 6—the one about comparing ourselves
with someone else (6:4), and the other concerning our need to
carry our own load (6:5). We are not to compare ourselves with
others, because we are to carry our own load. That is, we each
have our own obligation to measure up to God's standard for

us. In this light, comparison with others becomes out of the question.

It is also evident that this way of understanding the two seemingly contradictory commands about burden bearing— bearing each other's burdens (Galatians 6:2) and bearing our own burden (6:5)—relieves any supposed tension between them. We must bear the burden of sin that the sinning brother carries by helping to restore him to forgiveness and fellowship with Christ. And we must help our brother to bear any other burden that falls upon him from the hand of God. But we must also bear alone our own burden of fulfilling the standard of behavior that God has suited to us as individuals.[5]

Ministry to Christian Leaders (6:6)

The community of believers has an obligation to support its leaders in a tangible and material way. Throughout the whole of his long ministry Paul espoused this principle, upholding it even in one of his last letters when he exhorted Timothy:

> The elders who direct the affairs of the church well are worthy of double honor, especially those whose work is preaching and teaching. For the Scripture says, "Do not muzzle the ox while it is treading out the grain," and "The worker deserves his wages." (1 Timothy 5:17-18)

While Paul consistently recognized this obligation on the part of the taught, it is also true that he did not always avail himself of the privilege of such support, but more regularly sought to support himself, that he might not be a burden to those he ministered to or that impure and mercenary motives not be attributed to him. For example, he makes this point in his discussion with the Corinthians regarding the occasional need to curtail one's freedoms for the sake of ministering the gospel to others (1 Corinthians 9:3-15). And to the Thessalonians he writes:

> We loved you so much that we were delighted to share with you not only the gospel of God but our lives as well, because you had become so dear to us. Surely you remember, brothers, our toil and hardship; we worked night and day in order not to be a burden to anyone while we preached the gospel of God to you. (1 Thessalonians 2:8-9)

However, on occasion, he could employ in his own ministry the rule concerning the right of church leaders to financial support and was certainly glad to commend the Philippians for their generous contributions to him.

> Moreover, as you Philippians know, in the early days of your acquaintance with the gospel, when I set out from Macedonia, not one church shared with me in the matter of giving and receiving, except you only; for even when I was in Thessalonica, you sent me aid again and again when I was in need. (Philippians 4:15-16)

Paul could accept financial aid when it was appropriate, but he could be stubbornly scrupulous about not giving any impression of mercenary motives or behavior.

The Lord Himself endorsed the principle of the minister's right to benefit materially from those under His care when He, as teacher, received support from His followers (Luke 8:3). And He instructed His apostles to accept such benevolence from the towns and villages of Galilee in which they ministered (Matthew 10:9-10).

Ministry to All (Galatians 6:7-10)

It is difficult to see where the shift takes place from material support of leaders to ministry in material things that is directed toward all. But clearly the latter is in mind by 6:10, where Paul instructs his readers to "do good to all people, especially to those who belong to the family of believers." To see the shift taking place at 6:7 is certainly not objectionable.

And in the present context, doing good probably does refer primarily to help of a material nature, although that is but a particular application of the goodness in general that Paul had already described as a product of the Holy Spirit in the believer's life (5:22).

While this kind of ministry should be extended to all in need, as opportunities arise, such a ministry does not entirely leave believers out of the picture; they are, after all, part of the "all people" (6:10). In fact, there is even a priority given to this kind of ministry when its recipients are fellow believers ("especially").

Further, ministry through material means should be generous, as the whole context shows, and persistent. "Let us *not become weary* in doing good," he says, "for at the proper time we will reap a harvest *if we do not give up*" (6:9, emphasis added).

The New Testament provides us with abundant examples of this kind of ministry. Even Paul had been on both the giving end and the receiving end of material assistance. It was his desire to organize the collection of funds to assist the poverty-stricken church in Jerusalem, and one of the communities of Gentile Christians that contributed so heartily to this task was the group of churches throughout the province of Macedonia and the church at Philippi in particular.

But the practice of material assistance was far broader than the interests of the great apostle to the Gentiles. As far back as the early days of the gospel in Jerusalem the Church saw the need for assisting those of its number who were in material need (Acts 2:44-45; 4:32-37). While the precise form this assistance took in the early Church as it is described in the book of Acts may not necessarily supply the model to be followed for all time in the future, the principles are clearly applicable to issues of Christian benevolence and generosity.

Although it seems probable that the primary emphasis of this section is on the need for supplying material contribution, it may be useful to broaden the application to include all kinds of ministry, both to the people of God and to those outside the pale of the Christian community.

There is a heartwarming true story told by Mel Trotter[6] about a young boy who lived at the turn of the century in a slum section of Grand Rapids known as Bucktown. It seems that this Jimmie Moore, a lad still short of his teenage years, had been instructed by his sick and dying father to fetch the superintendent from the Mission, so that the father might hear more clearly the truth of the gospel. The result was that this superintendent, Mr. Morton, was able to lead both the father and young Jimmie, as well as other members of the family, to saving faith in Christ.

Immediately, Jimmie Moore took his simple faith in Jesus seriously. For him Jesus was his friend, who loved him and who would help him in any of life's experiences. But Jimmie saw this as a message not only for himself but also for all the inhabitants of Bucktown, and he proceeded to spread the message of Jesus' love and transforming power to nearly everyone he met. It mattered not to him to what depths a person had fallen—crime, drunkenness, prostitution—whatever it was, Jesus could help that person. Thus through this simple faith and the ministry it encouraged, many of the outcasts of society who came in contact with Jimmie Moore were brought into the family of God and to some extent, at least, delivered from lives of suffering.[7]

Conclusion

As practical as the teachings of this section are, it is not without theological interest as well. From such a perspective, the key issue in this paragraph is whether Paul is here teaching a doctrine of salvation (eternal life) by works. Of course, such a reading of the passage would not make a great deal of sense, especially in this letter, where Paul has been so meticulous to contradict that doctrine. Rather, Paul means that true saving faith is never found apart from practical works of love, so that to the extent that there are no works of love, to that extent there is no saving faith, and to the extent that there is no saving faith, to that extent there is no eternal life.

On the other hand, in spite of this theological significance, there is no question but that the predominant impact of the section is a practical one. In short, we should be as Dorcas, "always doing good and helping the poor" in practical ways, though not necessarily in the particular way she did, which was apparently to make clothing for the needy (Acts 9:36, 39).

And, of course, this obligation to minister materially to those in need is only truly fulfilled when such ministry comes from the heart and springs from the giving of oneself (2 Corinthians 8:1-5; 9:6-7). Nor is it a question of the amount of the gift, as the story of the widow's mite reminds us (Luke 21:2-4).

As to the emphasis that such material ministry as we have been considering does not exclude the family of believers, we have only to look at the practice of the early Church in Jerusalem to see how clearly this obligation was embraced. In particular, look to Barnabas, who "sold a field he owned and brought the money and put it at the apostles' feet" for distribution to the less fortunate members of the body of Christ (Acts 4:36-37).

Moreover, while we have these excellent positive examples in Scripture of what it means to minister to those in need, we also have the awesome case of the unnamed rich man, who refused help to the obviously needy Lazarus (Luke 16:19-21). Can we learn from the negative examples as well? But however we learn the truth, may God help us to help others.

> We give Thee but Thine own, whate'er the gift may
>   be;
> All that we have is Thine alone, a trust, O Lord, from
>   Thee.
>   May we Thy bounties thus as stewards true receive,
>   And gladly, as Thou blessest us, to Thee our first
>   fruits give.
> Oh, hearts are bruised and dead, and homes are bare
>   and cold,
> And lambs for whom the Shepherd bled are straying
>   from the fold.
>   To comfort and to bless, to find a balm for woe—
>   To tend the lone and fatherless is angels' work
>   below.
> The captive to release, to God the lost to bring,
> To teach the way of life and peace—it is a Christlike
>   thing.
>   And we believe Thy Word, though dim our faith
>   may be—
>   Whate'er for Thine we do, O Lord, we do it unto
>   Thee.[8]

Questions for Reflection or Discussion

1. When is it right and when wrong to think that we are something (Galatian 6:3) or take pride in ourselves (6:4)?

2. How does the word "for" in 6:5 help relate the rest of 6:5 to 6:2?

3. What is "the word" in which we may receive instruction (6:6)?

4. What is the destruction in mind in 6:8?

5. What is an "opportunity" (6:10)?

6. What is implied in the reference to the "family of believers" (6:10)?

Endnotes

1. The passage offers a valuable illustration, even though it is probably not an original part of the Fourth Gospel.

2. Compare also the ordinary kind of burden resulting from human existence that is implied in Matthew 20:12.

3. If burden bearing is interpreted more narrowly as referring specifically to restoration of a fallen believer, the law of Christ may be the kind of teaching found in Matthew 18:15-17.

4. See chapter 1.

5. This explanation of the difference between verses 2 and 5 is more natural than that which appeals to supposed distinctions between the two Greek words for burden.

6. Melvin E. Trotter, *Jimmie Moore of Bucktown* (New York: Fleming H. Revell Company, 1904).

7. Trotter says in his Preface, "All the characters here represented, though six years ago considered hopeless outcasts, are today prosperous, happy, contented citizens of Grand Rapids, and are living, breathing examples of the transforming power of Jesus Christ, with the glad story of Redemption on their lips every day. The transformation of Bucktown is civic history and the work in that locality has spread to every other locality in this city. Districts that were given over to drunkenness and fights and that were dependent upon benevolent organizations for existence are today self-supporting."

8. William W. How, "We Give Thee But Thine Own," *Hymns of the Christian Life* (Camp Hill, PA: Christian Publications, 1978), #223.

13

The Glory of Paul's Gospel

Galatians 6:11-18

See what large letters I use as I write to you with my own hand!

Those who want to make a good impression outwardly are trying to compel you to be circumcised. The only reason they do this is to avoid being persecuted for the cross of Christ. Not even those who are circumcised obey the law, yet they want you to be circumcised that they may boast about your flesh. May I never boast except in the cross of our Lord Jesus Christ, through which the world has been crucified to me, and I to the world. Neither circumcision nor uncircumcision means anything; what counts is a new creation. Peace and mercy to all who follow this rule, even to the Israel of God.

Finally, let no one cause me trouble, for I bear on my body the marks of Jesus.

The grace of our Lord Jesus Christ be with your spirit, brothers. Amen.

In closing the epistle, Paul apparently takes the pen in his hand personally (6:11) to inscribe what must then surely be considered the elements of his gospel that are of the utmost importance to him. He has done this in other letters as well (1 Corinthians 16:21-24; Colossians 4:18; 2 Thessalonians 3:17-18). In fact, in Second Thessalonians he implies that there is some kind of personal greeting in all his letters (3:17). Thus, for example, we might see the personal inscription in First Thessalonians to be the last verse (1 Thessalonians 5:28) or the last paragraphs (5:25-28). But apparently no other letter of his contains a personal inscription to the extent that we find it here in the epistle to the Galatians.

This note implies, of course, that the majority of the letter had been dictated by Paul to another, who actually did the physical writing. And indeed this is supported by the fact that occasionally the name of the scribe is given, as, for example, in Romans 16:22, where the scribe's name is Tertius.

But to say these things is by no means to detract from the letter's inspiration and authority. Divine inspiration comes at the point of composing the words, not at the point of moving the pen. The book of Galatians, along with all the books of the Old and New Testament canon, is fully the product of God's superintending Spirit, as well as being fully the composition of a human author.

The language Paul uses concerning the size of the letters is also of interest. It may imply a difficulty in vision, something that may also have been implied earlier when he talked about his illness and the willingness of the Galatians to give their own eyes to Paul (Galatians 4:13-15).

So Paul brings his letter to the Galatians to an end by harking back to the basics—the cross of Christ, the glory of the gospel. If on the subjective side of salvation, faith is the most basic concept, surely on the objective side the most basic is the cross of Christ and all that it represents.

In developing this theme he talks first about those who would debase the cross by making other considerations more important. Whatever might be their motive, the effect of their procedure is to demean and debase the cross itself. Then he moves on to consider what it means to embrace the cross, both enduring its offense and enjoying its benefits.

Debasing the Cross (6:12-13)

The clear outward action attributed to Paul's opponents, the false teachers, is that of trying to insist on the circumcision of these Gentile converts. But this was apparently accompanied by a willingness to tone down the proclamation of the crucified Messiah by way of subordinating it to other concerns. Circumcision had replaced the cross as the central feature of their proclamation.

Naturally, when we speak of the false teachers' opposition to the cross, we need to recognize that the objection is not merely to the cross as the particular form of the Messiah's death that was offensive. It was apparently the death of the Messiah itself to which they objected.

When Paul then addresses the question of the motives of these Judaizing teachers, he does so in a most devastating way: they want to make a good impression on someone and to avoid the persecution that accompanies a faithful preaching of a crucified Messiah (6:12). Apparently, Paul sees the false teachers as so eager to maintain good relations with the nonbelieving Jews that they are willing to compromise the gospel by propounding Gentile circumcision and correspondingly playing down the centrality of the cross.

But even in their insistence on having the Galatians circumcised they are not being entirely consistent with their own standards. Although they are emphasizing one law, the law of circumcision, they display a corresponding lack of concern for other aspects of the law (6:13). They do not obey it fully. Paul may have in mind the law of neighbor-love, which the false teachers were sadly neglecting in their treatment of the Galatians.

Moreover, Paul not only considers them inconsistent with their own principles about law; they are, in their willingness to play down the cross, also and more significantly inconsistent with the fundamental truth of the gospel. One cannot consistently be truly Christian and at the same time challenge so central a tenet of the Christian faith as the Messiah's death on a cross.

Paul's words come as a warning to us as well. Even as in the opening section of the letter, here we are confronted once again with the seriousness of distorting the gospel—a challenge that we must ever take with utter seriousness.

First, an unbalanced and distorted emphasis in our preaching of the gospel may even blind us to the unconscious or subconscious motives that may underlie such a distortion. Motives can be subtle, and it is doubtful whether Paul's opponents would have seen their motives as clearly as Paul thought he did.

Further, the pressure that we may feel from the culture around us to truncate the gospel by removing the scandal of the cross is particularly present in the modern era and manifests itself in many and subtle forms. Why, we are asked, would God kill His own beloved Son? And have we not in this modern age outgrown the need to think of a bloody sacrifice as a means of atonement? And do we really want to think that God is in need of being appeased with any kind of act, bloody or not, that could be taken as a sort of bribe? Isn't that a pagan idea? On and on the questions go. Our culture simply does not like the biblical concept of the atonement. Like the Jews and Gentiles of Paul's day, modern man is also offended by the cross of Christ.

But if there is anything that should characterize an authentic Christianity, it is fidelity to the preaching of the cross, no matter what the personal cost. It cannot be evaded; and when there is the attempt to avoid the offense of the cross, the cross itself and its significance for the believer are thereby cheapened and demeaned in the process. The cross is the glory of the gospel, not its embarrassment.

Embracing the Cross (6:14-18)

Embracing the cross is simply the opposite of debasing the cross. Embracing the cross is, as Paul calls it, glorying in the cross, and this involves both enduring its offense and enjoying its benefits.

Enduring its offense (6:14)

The cross and a crucified Messiah are an offense to both Jews and non-Jews. The majority of the Jews of Paul's day espoused a view of the Messiah that so emphasized His coming in triumph over Israel's enemies that His suffering and death were thereby precluded. To this kind of position the message of the cross was an offense.

And the cultured Gentile could likewise scarcely understand the concept of a religious teacher who had been subjected to the criminal penalty of crucifixion. So as long as Christianity is tied to a crucified Savior, it will necessarily meet with misunderstanding and resistance, and the proclaimers of such a message will be rejected and even possibly persecuted.

Let the cross, says Paul, bring persecution and discomfort. He had experienced these in abundance as effects of his preaching. But it did not matter, for to him there was a clear line separating him from the standards of the world, and that line was a shadow, as it were, cast by the cross of the Savior. It was by the cross that the world had been crucified to Paul and Paul to the world.

Likewise, the history of the Church is replete with stories of individuals who have similarly stood fast, even to the point of enduring death for the Lord who died for them. One example of such an individual was a student of the beloved disciple, John, by the name of Polycarp, who became the Bishop of the churches of Smyrna. The story of his fidelity to the cause of Christ is recorded in a letter written by someone in the Smyrnean church recounting Polycarp's martyrdom in the middle of the second century.

The account contains many interesting details, but it is enough for our purposes to indicate that after his arrest he was given opportunity, as was customary, to recant in the form of swearing by the fortune of Caesar, declaring "Caesar is Lord," offering incense, or cursing Christ. All of these Polycarp refused to do. His own words speak to his devotion to his Savior: "Eighty-six years I have served him, and he never did me any wrong. How can I blaspheme my King who saved me?"

While the actual word "cross" does not appear in this simple profession of faith, it is clear that Polycarp could never compromise that central tenet of his faith, that Christ had saved him by means of His death upon the cross to atone for sin.

And so may it be for us. Perhaps it will not for most of us come to such an extreme form of momentous choice as that which confronted the saintly Polycarp. But our fidelity to the Christ of the cross should be no less firm in the subtle challenges that we might face to compromise our allegiance to our Lord and Savior.

Enjoying its benefits (6:15-18)

Instead of the cross being a stumbling block to Paul, it was for him the glory of the gospel, the only thing in which he could legitimately boast. Nothing else counted for him. It offers benefits available from no other source.

The cross is the only means by which we can be constituted a new creation in Christ. As Paul says elsewhere: "to us who are being saved it [the message of the cross] is the power of God" (1 Corinthians 1:18).

Further, the result of following Paul's gospel of glorying in the cross is peace and mercy (Galatians 6:16), and in the sequel benediction, grace (6:18). True, the gospel also derives from God's grace, but here the thought is the continuation of that grace in the believer's life, clearly then a benefit resulting from embracing the cross.

In addition, those who follow Paul in believing the gospel are also called the Israel of God. In view of the general importance of names in Scripture, any name favorably given by God can be thought of as a benefit to be enjoyed by the recipient.

But what precisely does Paul mean by the term "Israel of God" (6:16)? It appears best to see in it a designation of Christians, the Church, the new people of God, and therefore as in some sense a new Israel or true Israel.

It is true that some interpreters see in this phrase an additional group alongside Jew and Gentile, along the lines of Paul's remark to the Corinthians: "Do not cause anyone to stumble, whether Jews, Greeks or the church of God" (1 Corinthians 10:32). But it is better to accept the NIV handling ("*even* . . . the Israel of God," Galatians 6:16), taking the phrase in apposition to the preceding one. According to this interpretation, we may fairly hold that Paul's meaning here is that those who adhere to the gospel of God are capable of being thought of as a true Israel, God's Israel.

The support for this idea does not come from this passage alone; it has parallels in other Pauline passages as well as others outside his writings. For example, Paul can call the overwhelmingly Gentile church at Philippi "the circumcision," taking a title that would be characteristic of Israel and applying it to the Church (Philippians 3:3).[1]

Furthermore, the same kind of thought appears to be present, at least implicitly, in Jesus' claim to be the true vine (John 15:1), that is, the true Israel. It is obvious from the context that the true vine incorporates within it also the branches that are found attached to it. Thus the passage is another virtual claim that the whole body of believers constitutes the true Israel.

And along the same line, Peter can say to largely Gentile Christians: "You are a chosen people, a royal priesthood, a holy nation, a people belonging to God" (1 Peter 2:9). While these phrases are not an exact replication of the terms God applied to Israel in Exodus 19:5-6, they are an obvious paraphrase of them. So again we can conclude that the New Testament in general supports this idea that the church is a new or true Israel.[2]

The point naturally has far-reaching theological implications for seeing the body of Christ as the heir of fundamental Old Testament promises. The Church is now Jehovah's wife.[3] And it is the Church that carries on Israel's role as God's witness to the world.[4]

On the other hand, such an interpretation of the Church as a new Israel does not do away with the fulfillment of God's promise in the nation of Israel. For Paul clearly announces a large-scale conversion of ethnic Israel when he says (Romans 11:26-27): "All Israel will be saved, as it is written: 'The deliverer will come from Zion; he will turn godlessness away from Jacob. And this is my covenant with them when I take away their sins.' "

Yes, there is a future for ethnic Israel, but this truth in no way prohibits our holding also that the New Testament writers treat the Church as a true Israel.

We must admit, however, that these writers seem to be a bit reserved on this subject since such a conclusion is more implied in the way they use terms than explicitly stated. Nevertheless, it does not seem objectionable to make the point explicit in our theological expression, as long as one does not take the final step and rule out a significant future for ethnic Israel.

This identification of the Church as God's new Israel is not simply an academic issue but carries with it some practical consequences as well. For the believer may thereby find solace in the fact of being God's chosen, the object of His loving delight. But such status is also one of obligation—the awesome responsibility of being God's witness in a sin-darkened and needy world.

Conclusion

It is no exaggeration to say that in Paul's thinking Christ is central to redemption and that the cross is central to an adequate understanding of Christ. We rightly believe that Christ is the center, that in Him "are hidden all the treasures of wisdom and knowledge" (Colossians 2:3), that Christ is our life (3:4), that He has become for us wisdom from God—that is, our righteousness, holiness and redemption (1 Corinthians 1:30). He is all and in all (Colossians 3:11). Small wonder, then, that A.B. Simpson could write: "Everything in Jesus, and Jesus everything."[5]

But not only is Christ Himself the center of our faith; the cross and the corresponding resurrection and ascension are the central realities of the Christ event. Everything we have in redemption is somehow traceable to the cross. There is no deeper life apart from the cross, and any deeper Christian life that exists is at the heart of the matter but a deeper attachment to the cross. "We preach Christ crucified" (1 Corinthians 1:23).

When we speak of the cross, it is, of course, not the physical entity but rather the Savior who died on the cross for our sins. That is, it is the cross that is a symbol of God's system of atonement.

Liberal theology in general has sought to deny the biblical concept of atonement while retaining the cross as a symbol of some other feature of Christian belief. But however high and beautiful a symbolism liberalism offered to interpret the cross, it turned out to be not the biblical symbolism but a pale substitute. How could any system that denied, or at least radically reinterpreted, the reality of sin need the biblical system of atonement? It becomes entirely unnecessary in the sense of there being a Savior taking the place of the sinner and paying the penalty for the sinner's transgression. If there is no real need for a Savior, the cross becomes a symbol of God's love—love intended to influence us to follow God. According to this view, we need to follow the Lord, whatever the cost, just as Jesus followed His Father, though it cost Him His life.

This liberal construction of the gospel is far from Paul's thinking. His gospel is one of Jesus dying in our place, as our substitute, to remove our sin and its penalty. All of these ideas are in Paul's mind when he talks about the cross. His is a biblical theology, not a liberal theology.

These two perspectives can be graphically portrayed by a comparison of the life and thought of two men of approximately the same vintage: Harry Emerson Fosdick, the quintessential liberal, and the proverbial conservative John Gresham Machen.

It is interesting that Fosdick was raised in substantially the same kind of evangelical Christian faith as was Machen. But in his mature years Fosdick rejected the authority of Scripture and substituted a highly psychological and developmental interpretation of faith. Machen, on the other hand, while struggling for a time with the very same issues as Fosdick, chose to remain faithful to the Scriptures, and therefore faithful to its gospel of the cross.

Fosdick became famous, pastoring influential Baptist churches in New York City and living a long and productive life popularizing his liberal version of the gospel. Machen's career was cut short by premature death. His name was not nearly the household word Fosdick's once was. His fame is virtually nonexistent outside the circles of evangelical Christianity.

Yet it is Machen who will on that great day receive the commendation, "Well done, good and faithful servant" (Matthew

25:21, 23), because it is he who preached the message of the cross. Let us likewise be faithful.

A similar pair from an earlier generation and, to be sure, more pastoral than professorial, consists of Lyman Abbott and A.B. Simpson, both preachers at influential churches in New York City around the turn of the century.

Lyman Abbott was a popular representative of what was then called the New Theology. New Theology tried to reinterpret the New Testament teaching in categories deemed suitable for modern thought. Even the title of his main expression of this attempt, *Theology of an Evolutionist*, is revealing. In it he maintained:

> We believe not in the propitiation of an angry God by another suffering to appease the Father's wrath, but in the perpetual self-propitiation of the Father, whose mercy, going forth to redeem from sin, satisfies as nothing else could the divine indignation against sin, by abolishing it.[6]

As far as Abbott is concerned, God simply does away with His wrath at sin. He ceases to be angry with sinners and their rebellious deeds. This is a far cry from the New Testament's teaching concerning the substitutionary death of Christ in which the Redeemer takes the place of the sinner in order to avert God's wrath against the sinner's sin. It is indeed a new theology, not the one taught in the pages of Holy Scripture.

On the other hand, A.B. Simpson remained ever faithful to the historic understanding of the atonement as one in which the Savior takes the place of the sinner and pays the penalty that is due for the sin committed. Simpson was well aware of the difference between the biblical teaching and the new perspective. He says this:

The very foundation of Christianity is the Gospel of the cross. Take that away and we have nothing left but a scheme of philosophy and morals. But alas, in the craze for novelty, religious leaders are growing weary of the old story and they invent a new doctrine of the cross. They tell us that Jesus Christ died not to atone for the sins of men, or bear our guilt and stand beneath the judgment of God as our Substitute and Sacrifice for sin, but simply that He might inspire other men to live a similar life of sacrifice for their fellows. The atonement, according to these wild weavers of the spider's web of the New Theology, is simply learning to imitate the self-sacrifice of the Lord Jesus and, like Him, give our lives for our fellowmen. Is it too much to say that such a caricature of Calvary and Christianity crucifies afresh the Son of God, and puts Him to an open shame?[7]

What is most interesting in connection with these attempts to water down the glory of the cross is that some of the proponents of the modernist interpretations seemed to entertain second thoughts about their doctrines as their own death approached. For example, Horace Bushnell, the modern father of the New Theology's reinterpretation of the atonement, is reported to have said at the end of his life, "I fear what I have written and said upon the moral idea of the atonement is misleading and will do great harm. . . . Oh Lord Jesus, I trust for mercy only in the shed blood that thou didst offer on Calvary."[8]

According to Paul, the cross is not merely a demonstration of the Father's love or a supreme act of love and devotion on the part of the Son, although indeed it is all of this. But it is much more. The true significance of the cross of Christ is the shedding of His blood for the remission of sins. That is the glory of the cross.

When I survey the wondrous cross
   on which the Prince of glory died,
My richest gain I count but loss,
   and pour contempt on all my pride.

Forbid it, Lord, that I should boast,
   save in the death of Christ my God;
All the vain things that charm me most,
   I sacrifice them to His blood.

See, from His head, His hands, His feet,
   sorrow and love flow mingled down—
Did e'er such love and sorrow meet,
   or thorns compose so rich a crown?

Were the whole realm of nature mine,
   that were a present far too small;
Love so amazing, so divine,
   demands my soul, my life, my all.[9]

Questions for Reflection or Discussion

1. How would Paul's opponents be able to boast about the Galatians' flesh (Galatians 6:13)?
2. How is the world crucified (6:14)?
3. How is Paul's crucifixion to the world (6:14) related to 2:20 and 5:24?
4. Who would cause Paul trouble (6:17)? What trouble would they cause (6:17)?
5. What does Paul mean by the Galatians' "spirit" with which Paul wants Christ's grace to be present (6:18)?

Endnotes

1. That the Philippian church was predominantly Gentile is shown by the fact that when Paul arrived at the city, there were not enough Jews living there to meet in a synagogue, so that he found them assembled in the open air by the river (see Acts 16:13). Furthermore, Paul's "we" in the Philippians passage must include his readers, since it would be counter-productive in this context to be emphasizing that only Jewish believers are the true circumcision. Thus the passage is saying that the Church is the true circumcision, which is but a step from saying that the Church is the true Israel.
2. The largely Gentile nature of Peter's readers is implied in First Peter 4:4; pagans would not think it particularly strange if *Jews* did not "plunge with them into the same flood of dissipation." But if former pagans ceased engaging in their former licentious activities, that would seem strange.
3. It would be overly pedantic to insist on a distinction between Jehovah's wife, implied in Hosea 2:19 and the wife of the Lamb (Revelation 21:9).
4. Compare Isaiah 43:10 and Acts 1:8.
5. A.B. Simpson, "Himself," *Hymns of the Christian Life* (Camp Hill, PA: Christian Publications, 1978), # 248.
6. Quoted in Augustus Hopkins Strong, *Systematic Theology* (New York: Fleming H. Revell Company, 1907), 739.
7. A.B. Simpson, *The Cross of Christ* (Camp Hill, PA: Christian Publications, Inc., 1910), 65-66.
8. Quoted in Strong, 739.
9. Isaac Watts, "When I Survey the Wondrous Cross," *Hymns of the Christian Life* (Camp Hill, PA: Christian Publications, 1978), # 82.

Select Bibliography

Bruce, Frederick F. *The Epistle to the Galatians: A Commentary on the Greek Text*. Grand Rapids: William B. Eerdmans Publishing Company, 1982.

Fung, Ronald Y.K. *The Epistle to the Galatians*. Grand Rapids: William B. Eerdmans Publishing Company, 1988.

Lightfoot, John B. *Saint Paul's Epistle to the Galatians*. London: Macmillan and Co., 1921.

Longenecker, Richard N. *Galatians*. Dallas: Word Books, Publisher, 1990.

Morris, Leon. *Galatians: Paul's Charter of Christian Freedom*. Downers Grove: InterVarsity Press, 1996.

Silva, Moises. *Explorations in Exegetical Method: Galatians as a Test Case*. Grand Rapids: Baker Books, 1996.